SURRENDER

The Secret to Perfect Peace & Happiness

Eusebio Blough

SURRENDER

The Secret to Perfect Peace & Happiness

Gregory L. Jackson, Sr.

REVIEW AND HERALD® PUBLISHING ASSOCIATION
HAGERSTOWN, MD 21740

The author assumes full responsibility for the accuracy of all facts and quotations as cited in this book.

This book was
Edited by Richard W. Coffen
Designed by Patricia S. Wegh
Cover design by Mark O'Connor
Typeset: 11.5/13.5 Palatino

PRINTED IN U.S.A.

98 97 96 95 94 5 4 3 2 1

Library of Congress Cataloging in Publication Data
Jackson, Gregory L., 1949–
Surrender: the secret to perfect peace and happiness / Gregory L. Jackson, Sr.
p. cm.
Includes bibliographical references.

1. Spiritual life—Seventh-day Adventists. 2. Freedom (Theology) 3. God—Will. 4. Seventh-day Adventists—Doctrines. 5. Adventists—Doctrines. 6. Sabbatarians—Doctrines. I. Title.
BV4501.2.J31254 1994
248.4'86732—dc20
94-27759
CIP

ISBN 0-8280-0733-0

Dedication

I dedicate this book to
my grandfather, Shelton E. Kilby, Sr.
His spiritual guidance and profound love for
the Lord, the Word, and the church
have made a tremendous impact on my life
and have greatly influenced the shaping
of many of the ideas
I share in this book.

Acknowledgments

Nothing worthwhile is ever done alone. There are many contributors to any positive accomplishments. This book is a positive accomplishment for me—an accomplishment that would not have been what it is without the help of

my family: especially my three sons, who have put up with me and loved me through it all.
my mother: who gave me a healthy concept of God's unconditional love for me because of her own tremendous love. (Mother, I even appreciate your insistence on my use of correct English! I see the importance now.)
my friends: Fred Willis, whom God used to inspire me to write this book, and Charlotte Thoms, whose company, With These Hands Ministries, helped me fine-tune my manuscript before I submitted it.
my God: who not only made it all possible but more importantly makes it possible for me to enjoy a life of perfect peace and happiness.

Contents

Preface

For the preaching of the cross is to them that perish foolishness; but unto us which are saved it is the power of God (I Cor. 1:18).

Ever since Adam and Eve doubted God and ate from the tree of the knowledge of good and evil, human beings have been on an endless quest to find peace and happiness, but in the wrong way. Like Eve, we somehow believe that we are missing something when we don't partake of this world's forbidden fruit. Even sincere Christians are sometimes inclined to think this way. Why else would Paul say in Colossians 2:8-10: "Beware lest any man spoil you through philosophy and vain deceit, after the tradition of men, after the rudiments of the world, and not after Christ. For in him dwelleth all the fulness of the Godhead bodily. And ye are complete in him, which is the head of all principality and power."

The term *complete* means "to lack nothing." Contrary to everything we have been taught and may feel or believe, the only way to perfect peace and fulfillment is found in Christ. David said it this way: "The Lord is my shepherd; I shall not want" (Ps. 23:1). Notice that David did not say "I shall not *need.*" Instead, he said "I shall not *want.*" This contradicts the popular saying that goes, "God promised to satisfy our needs, not our wants [meaning our desires]." Many people, including

Christians, feel the want of many things. Perhaps you're one of them. You may even feel you need some things. Well, I've got good news for you. God cannot lie, and He promises that when you allow Him to be your shepherd, you will not want—or lack—*anything.*

Most of us know that this is what the Bible says. Why is it, then, that those who profess to follow the Lord often seem to feel that they not only want but also need so much? Can you actually live in a constant state of *not* wanting? If so, how? Is it possible to find perfect peace and happiness in this present world?

The purpose of this book is to show that the answer to these questions is a resounding *yes!* The reason so many Christians don't have perfect peace and happiness is that they don't really understand how to put into practice Luke 9:23, in which Jesus said: "If any man will come after me, let him deny himself, and take up his cross daily, and follow me."

I must confess that I too have struggled with Jesus' admonition to lift my cross daily. Many days I've even refused to do so. This was because I didn't really have the right understanding of what it actually meant to lift my cross. It has been through much pain, disappointment, agonizing prayer, and many hours of study that God has taught me the true meaning and blessing of daily lifting my cross. Now I look forward to my "daily lift," because I have found the truth expressed in this statement: "As we lift this cross we shall find that it lifts us" (Ellen G. White, *Testimonies,* vol. 8, p. 45).

If you have been struggling with your daily lift, if your cross has been too hard for you to bear, if you want to know what it feels like to be complete and to want nothing, if you want to know how to experience perfect peace and happiness continually, then this book is for you.

Chapter One

What Is the Cross Experience?

I protest by your rejoicing which I have in Christ Jesus our Lord, I die daily (I Cor. 15:31).

While pastoring in the Dayton, Ohio, area I was talking to one of my parishioners about how she could be an effective witness for the Lord. To my surprise, she began to protest vehemently by saying, "I can't do that. I don't know how."

After a few minutes of further conversation, I realized that her protest resulted from what she thought I meant by the word "witness." To her, a witness was someone who could give a formal Bible study or someone who could quote Scripture like one of the apostles. When I explained that by witnessing I meant simply telling someone else what the Lord had done for her, she breathed a deep sigh of relief and said, "Oh, I can do that."

Many people know what the Bible *says*. However, precious few rightly understand what the Bible *means*. And it isn't because the Bible is so hard to understand. An explanation for this may be found in 1 Corinthians 2:14: "But the natural man receiveth not the things of the Spirit of God: for they are foolishness unto him: neither can he know them, because they are spiritually discerned."

Some of you probably think that doesn't apply to good churchgoing Christians, but this is exactly to whom Paul was writing. Notice what he says in 1 Corinthians 3:1-3: "And I, brethren, could not speak unto you as unto spiritual, but as unto carnal, even as unto babes in Christ. I have fed you with milk, and not with meat: for hitherto ye were not able to bear it, neither yet now are ye able. For ye are yet carnal."

I fear that this statement still applies to most Christians today. In fact, it may be even more applicable in today's world. "This know also, that in the last days perilous times shall come. For men shall be lovers of their own selves, . . . having a form of godliness, but denying the power thereof: . . . ever learning, and never able to come to the knowledge of the truth" (2 Tim. 3:1-7).

The English word "knowledge" here translates the Greek word *epignosis*. It means more than the mere accumulation of facts; it means to perceive, to fully discern. Very few Christians fully discern the meaning of Luke 9:23: "If any man will come after me, let him deny himself, and take up his cross daily, and follow me." Like the Lord's disciples of old, our understanding of the cross has more to do with our traditions and worldly practices than with the truth. This does not mean that we aren't sincere Christians. It does mean, however, that we'll have to go through some bitter disappointments, heartaches, and pain before we are able to come to a knowledge of the truth, as did Jesus' original disciples. I decided to start with an explanation of the true meaning of the cross because I'm convinced that this is a topic most Christians don't understand.

To most people, the cross is very negative. Just the thought of it conjures up images of sadness, sacrifice, hard work, and toil. At best, we relate to it like children taking castor oil. We deal with it because we've been told we have to if we want to get better. So we take our medicine—bitter though it may be—by taking up our cross, because one day we'll receive a crown. When viewed like this, the cross becomes a burden. And in this world of burdens, who needs another one to lift? Isn't it enough that we have to carry the burdens of rearing a family, pleasing a demanding mate, finding and keeping a job, paying the bills, getting an education, staying healthy, and on and on and on? Must we lift the cross, too? But then we're told that "good" Christians don't complain. We're admonished, "Just 'be strong in the Lord' and lift your cross like a good soldier because no cross, no crown."

This concept of the cross, which is by far the most popular, leads to three different types of Christians. I've chosen to name the three types the Martyr, the Happy Christian, and the Happy Martyr.

The Martyr embraces the idea that the cross involves toil, sacrifice, heartache, and strife. Martyrs believe that one must endure hardness in order to earn heaven. They heartily endorse the saying "no cross, no crown." Martyrs believe that being solemn and serious is synonymous with righteousness. Therefore, anything that causes them to feel too happy and upbeat is suspect as being sinful. Their favorite theme revolves around "doing the Lord's work" and "sacrificing for the Lord." Thus testimonies of Martyrs usually consist of telling what he or she has "given up" or what he or she is "doing" for the Lord. Instead of praising the Lord for His goodness, Martyrs often focus on the hard times they're having or how much they're suffering, but in spite of it all, they're going to continue to be faithful. After all, God did say: "All that will live godly in Christ Jesus shall suffer persecution" (2 Tim. 3:12).

To the Martyr, the promises of joy, happiness, perfect peace, and material blessings are usually to be realized in the "sweet by and by." Now is the time for us to prove ourselves faithful through sacrifice, toil, and hard work. To this type of Christian, the daily lift becomes a task that must be done faithfully in order to earn heaven. This view of the cross causes one either to become proud and self-righteous about his or her works, or discouraged and dismayed at the lack of them.

Next we come to the *Happy Christian.* Happy Christians, too, believe that bearing the cross means toil, sacrifice, and sadness, but their response is totally different from that of the Martyrs. I would say that Happy Christians have developed as a reaction to the Martyrs.

They may have even tried cross-bearing religion for a while, but were totally disgusted with the outcome. Therefore, they reject the idea of lifting the cross daily. This rejection isn't so much in word as it is in the interpretation of and focus on certain scriptural passages.

For instance, Happy Christians emphasize the Lord's promises. They believe in receiving the reward right now. Happy Christians believe that God wants His children to live not a life of gloom and doom, but one of hope and faith. They don't believe that a Christian should have to sacrifice and toil for the Lord. Instead, a Christian is to receive and rejoice.

Happy Christians don't have heartache and strife, because they are too busy feeling the joy of the Lord. To this type of Christian, feeling good is synonymous with righteousness. Their music is happy and upbeat, and so are their testimonies. The Happy Christian must be on a high at all times, because anything that is not lively and upbeat doesn't have the Spirit in it and is, therefore, not of the Lord.

While all this sounds closer to what a Christian should be, there's one big problem. Everything is based on feelings. The Martyr believes in righteousness by works, but the Happy Christian believes in righteousness by feeling.

In order to illustrate the difference in focus and emphasis even further, I will show how each would interpret 1 John 5:14, 15, which says: "And this is the confidence that we have in him, that, if we ask any thing according to his will, he heareth us: and if we know that he hear us, whatsoever we ask, we know that we have the petitions that we desired of him."

Happy Christians will focus on the parts that make them feel good. They would put more emphasis on verse 15, saying, "The Lord says, 'Whatsoever we ask, we know that we have the petitions that we desired of him.'" Surely this will make a person feel good. It gives a formula that encourages Christians to use God's power to get whatever they desire. All they have to do is claim the promise and believe hard enough . . . and it *will* happen.

This approach makes faith a lot like Dorothy's shoes in *The Wizard of Oz.* All Dorothy had to do was to believe as she clicked the magical shoes together, and the wizard had to grant her wish. So Happy Christians go out and claim the car they have always wanted (or healing or whatever). If it does not happen the way they think it should or at the time they think it should, it is because their faith is faulty. Therefore they must try harder to believe.

It never occurs to Happy Christians that the problem could be in their interpretation of 1 John 5:14, 15. To them the promise is simple: "*Whatsoever* we ask."

By now the Martyrs are feeling very superior because they know the answer to the Happy Christians' dilemma. The problem is that they have failed to focus on the qualifying phrase in verse 14, which is "according to his will." To the Martyrs, the Christians' desires are lost sight of in light of the emphasis on God's omnipotent will.

Since the Martyrs' view of the cross is one of carrying

burdens, it's hard for them to perceive that God's will is ever something that will make life easier and happier. This is why Christians should not pray for material things, healing, and things like that. Maybe God will give these things sometimes, but only to be used in His work. To use them for one's own enjoyment is sin.

I have a problem with both the Martyrs' and the Happy Christians' interpretation of this passage of Scripture. The Martyrs tend to emphasize "according to his will" to the neglect of "whatsoever we desire," whereas the Happy Christians tend to exalt the "whatsoever we desire" above the "according to his will."

But before dealing with that, I must first deal with the third response—that of the *Happy Martyr.* Happy Martyrs can be easily described. They are a mixture of the Happy Christian and the Martyr. How much of a mixture depends on how far they are on the continuum between the two extremes. Let me illustrate this with a diagram.

Martyr—1—2—3—4—5—6—7—8—9—10—*Happy Christian*

On this diagram number 1 is pure Martyr, and 10 is pure Happy Christian.

The twos, threes, and fours are not pure Martyr, but tend to view life more from the Martyr's eyes. When unpleasant things happen, these people are more inclined to say, "This is the cross that I must bear" than they are to say "I rebuke that demon in the name of Jesus."

Turn that around, and you have your sevens, eights, and nines. And in the case of the fives and sixes, they can go both ways but usually express it differently. When they view things as the Martyr does, they say, "The Lord never puts on you more than you can bear." When they take the perspective of the Happy Christian, they say, "You know, the devil sure is busy!"

I believe there's room for the two to come together in such a way that shall both realize God's will and satisfy human desires. This can be accomplished only by having the right view or understanding of the *"daily lift."* But this cannot be done via the compromise I just described.

You see, I disagree with the basic philosophies of these three types of Christians because they are all based on the wrong understanding of what the cross really means. To each of these groups, the cross means something negative, unpleasant, and burdensome. But is this what Jesus wants us to lift every day in order to follow Him? Is this supposed to be our daily lift, and if not, what is?

The best place to start answering these questions is with the text that started it all. In Luke 9:23 Jesus said: "And he said to them all, If any man will come after me, let him deny himself, and take up his cross daily, and follow me."

To the Martyr I would say that the cross experience is not a call to sacrifice *something*—it is a call to sacrifice *someone,* and that someone is *you.* God does not need our money, for all the silver and gold are His. God does not need our time, for He inhabits eternity. God does not need our works, for without Him we can do nothing.

What God wants is to occupy first place in our hearts. He wants us to surrender all to Him—our will, our time, our energy, our plans, our desires, our goals, our loved ones—*all* to His control. He wants us to live totally for Him. This is what He meant when He said that one must take up the cross daily and follow Him. The cross is for dying, not for carrying. It is a symbol of dying to self so that God may have His rightful place in our lives. Before the cross experience, self is supreme; what we want is all that really matters. God only comes into the picture to help us accomplish what we desire. This is true even for the Martyr. His desire is to be *self*-righteous. When self is on the throne, faith becomes a tool to use God's power to get our selfish desires met.

Truly the cross experience calls for self-denial, but not as the Martyr sees it. Here is a very revealing statement for the Martyr: "We are not to make crosses for ourselves, by wearing sackcloth, by pinching our bodies, or by denying ourselves wholesome, nourishing food. . . . neither are we required to expose health and life unnecessarily, nor to go mourning up the hill of Christian life, feeling it a sin to be cheerful, contented, happy, and joyful. These are all self-made crosses, but not the cross of Christ" *(Testimonies,* vol. 4, pp. 626, 627).

Jesus was talking to all those who think like the Martyr when He said: "Come unto me, all ye that labour and are heavy laden, and I will give you rest. Take my yoke upon you, and learn of me; for I am meek and lowly in heart: and ye shall find rest unto your souls" (Matt. 11:28, 29).

This yoke represents the cross. "The yoke and the cross are symbols representing the same thing, the giving up of the will to God" *(The Seventh-day Adventist Bible Commentary,* Ellen G. White Comments, vol. 5, p. 1090). What Jesus is calling for in Luke 9:23 is total surrender of our wills to the will of God. This is what the daily lift is. This is what Jesus meant when He said to learn of Him, because this is how He lived. His testimony was: "I can of mine own self do nothing: as I hear, I judge: and my judgment is just; because I seek not mine own will, but the will of the Father which hath sent me" (John 5:30). "Jesus saith unto them, My meat is to do the will of him that sent me, and to finish his work" (John 4:34).

And what about Happy Christians? They emphasize human desires to the neglect of God's will. There is no cross experience or self-denial. Notice what Ellen White has to say in *The Acts of the Apostles:* "Holiness is not rapture: it is an entire surrender of the will to God; it is living by every word that proceeds from the mouth of God; it is doing the will of our heavenly Father" (p. 51).

To Happy Christians I would say that this text does bring out that we're to have a cross experience. *Holiness is not a feeling. It is a decision to follow the Lord wherever He leads, even if doing so doesn't make you feel good at the time.*

Jesus came in the "likeness of sinful flesh" (Rom. 8:3) not only to redeem us but also to set an example of how we are to live. His life is the perfect pattern that He expects us to follow. Jesus lived the cross experience, and the apostle Paul admonishes us to have the same mind in us (Phil. 2:5-8). When we have the mind of Christ, we will be surrendered to God, as He was. If anybody had a right to exalt himself, He did, because He was God. But He "made himself of no reputation, and took upon him the form of a servant, and was made in the likeness of men: and being found in fashion as a man, he humbled himself, and became obedient unto death, even the death of the cross" (verses 7, 8).

As a human, Jesus was so emptied of self that He would rather die, even the shameful death of the cross, than go against the Father's will. That's the kind of mindset one must have to follow Jesus all the way. This is why Paul said, "I die daily" (1 Cor. 15:31).

One can clearly see why this understanding of the cross can be hard for the Happy Christian to accept. It requires surrendering to God's will no matter how that surrender makes one feel at the time. But it isn't so evident how this understanding differs from the Martyr's point of view. Here's where the story of the rich young ruler, in Matthew 19:16-22, can help.

The rich young ruler was one of God's chosen people. He kept all God's commandments. More than that, he also kept the traditions of his faith. He gave alms to the poor, fasted at the required times, returned a faithful tithe, gave sacrificial offerings, and observed all the health laws. If he were alive today, he would faithfully attend Sabbath school, church, and prayer meeting. On top of all of this, he had everything done before sunset on Friday night.

All this—and more—he had done from his "youth up" (verse 20). According to the law and the writings of the prophets, he was blameless. Yet he didn't have the perfect peace that comes from having eternal life. Being of the Martyr mentality, he thought that this longing could be satisfied by doing some "good thing." So he ran to Jesus with this question: "Good Master, what good thing shall I *do*, that I may have eternal life?" (verse 16).

To every good Martyr, this is not only a legitimate question, but also a virtuous one. "After all," says the Martyr, "he wasn't asking for some material thing. Instead, he was willing to give up something material so that he might be assured of eternal life."

This may seem to be noble until you test his request by the right understanding of the cross. Then you can see the problem with the question What good thing must I do?

The young ruler saw good only in terms of doing something. Not only that, but he thought he could do that something by using his own strength, and this would earn him salvation. If he'd had a correct understanding of the cross, he would have realized he could never *do* anything to earn eternal life. The cross tells us we must stop doing and start surrendering so that the One who *is* good can work in us that which is good.

Notice how Jesus taught this truth to the young ruler. Jesus told him that goodness isn't a thing but a person, and that person is God (verse 17). Therefore, there was nothing he could do, apart from God, that was good. But Jesus knew that the young ruler couldn't yet grasp this reality, so He went on to say: "But if thou wilt enter into life, keep the commandments" (verse 17).

Jesus was now meeting the man at his belief level. He was talking Martyr language. But this answer only frustrated the young ruler, because he had been doing all these *good things,* and he still didn't have the peace he longed for. As he thought about what Jesus said, it began to dawn on him that there was nothing wrong with what he was doing. The problem was with *him.* He then cried out: "What lack I yet?" (verse 20).

Now Jesus has gotten his focus off doing things and on himself. He is now ready to be taught the correct understanding of the cross. "Jesus said unto him, If thou wilt be perfect, go and sell that thou hast, and give to the poor, and thou shalt have treasure in heaven: and come and follow me" (verse 21).

At first glance, it seems that Jesus was requiring him to do some good thing to earn eternal life. It seems as though the Martyr is right—the cross means you must sacrifice *something.* But is this really what Jesus was saying? Is there some good thing that we can do to inherit eternal life, and is that good thing to sell all we have and give the proceeds to the poor?

I think not. "And though I bestow all my goods to feed the poor, and though I give my body to be burned, and have not charity, it profiteth me nothing" (1 Cor. 13:3). This tells us that it's possible to do all that—and more—and still be lost.

Jesus wants much more than our material wealth. He wants even more than our physical bodies. Jesus wants *total control* of our lives. He wants not just part of the heart, but all of it. As long as the young ruler had his wealth, he'd never be fully surrendered to Christ. Oh, he'd be willing to give huge sums of money to God's cause or make many other sacrifices *as long as he main-*

tained control over certain areas of his life. But to give away all his wealth would require total surrender to the Lord's control. Without his money he'd be totally dependent on the Lord for everything.

"Christ gave this man a test. He called upon him to choose between the heavenly treasure and worldly greatness. The heavenly treasure was assured him if he would follow Christ. But self must yield; his will must be given into Christ's control. The very holiness of God was offered to the young ruler. He had the privilege of becoming a son of God, and a coheir with Christ to the heavenly treasure. But he must take up the cross, and follow the Saviour in the path of self-denial" (Ellen G. White, *The Desire of Ages,* pp. 519, 520).

"But when the young man heard that saying, he went away sorrowful: for he had great possessions" (Matt. 19:22).

This is the response many have when they discover what it takes to follow the Lord fully. When we realize that we must give the Lord control of our goals, our dreams, our careers, our appetites—everything in our lives—we feel that the Lord is asking too much of us. And like the rich young ruler, we go away sorrowful. We go back to being good Martyrs and Happy Christians, just as the young ruler went back to life as usual.

Now that we understand that the daily lift represents total surrender on a daily basis, we need to deal with some important questions. Why is it necessary to surrender *all* to follow the Lord? Doesn't He expect us to have some goals of our own? Doesn't He say that He will give us the desires of *our* hearts?

These questions and more will be dealt with in the next chapter.

Discussion Questions

1. What is the most popular belief concerning the meaning of the cross experience? (pp. 14, 15)

2. What are the three types of Christians that result from this [mis]understanding? (p. 15)

3. What verse does the Martyr emphasize when interpreting 1 John 5:14, 15? Why? (p. 17)

4. What verse does the Happy Christian emphasize when interpreting 1 John 5:14, 15? Why? (p. 17)

5. What is the problem with the Martyr's view? (pp. 17, 18)

6. What is the problem with the Happy Christian's view? (pp. 18, 19)

7. What does Jesus mean in Luke 9:23 when He says to take up your cross daily? (pp. 20, 21)

8. What texts of Scripture tell us that Jesus lived the cross experience? Explain. (p. 21)

9. What type of Christian would you say the rich young ruler was? Why? (pp. 21-22)

10. What did Jesus tell the rich young ruler he must do in order to be perfect? What was his response and why? (pp. 22-24)

Chapter Two

Why the Cross Is Necessary

The heart is deceitful above all things, and desperately wicked: who can know it? (Jer. 17:9).

In the previous chapter I stated that only the right view of the cross makes it possible for both the divine will and human desires to be satisfied. In this chapter, we'll find out why this is so as we deal with why the cross experience is necessary. Jeremiah 17:9 tells us that our greatest enemy is not the devil but our own "deceitful" and "desperately wicked" hearts.

Contrary to what we may believe and so often say, the devil cannot make us do anything we don't already desire to do. The Bible lets us know that temptation begins from within. "But every man is tempted, when he is drawn away of his own lust, and enticed" (James 1:14).

The word "lust" means desires. So James states that we are tempted when Satan is able to appeal to our desires. All Satan has to do is come up with something we like and present it in such a way that it appeals to our natural senses. After that, the rest of the work is done by our own wicked and deceitful hearts, with Satan acting as a cheerleader or as a yes-man, seconding every sinful emotion.

Jeremiah 17:9 reveals a truth about each of us that we don't like to admit, and that truth is that we *love* sin. It's the warp and woof of our nature.

David realized this after his escapade with Bathsheba, and he confessed: "Behold, I was shapen in iniquity; and in sin did my mother conceive me" (Ps. 51:5).

Isaiah had to be given a vision of the Lord sitting upon His throne, high and lifted up, before he could say "Woe is me! for I am undone; because I am a man of unclean lips, and I dwell in the midst of a people of unclean lips: for mine eyes have seen the King, the Lord of hosts" (Isa. 6:5).

Paul had to be knocked from his horse on the Damascus road and blinded for three days before he could see clearly enough to proclaim: "For we know that the law is spiritual: but I am carnal, sold under sin. . . . For I know that in me (that is, in my flesh,) dwelleth no good thing: for to will is present with me; but how to perform that which is good I find not" (Rom. 7:14-18).

We don't like to face this truth about ourselves. We like to believe that we're not so bad after all. We are like the Pharisee in Luke 18:10-14. We love to point out other people's faults and shortcomings because this makes us feel better about ourselves. We love to extol our virtues and hear others sing our praises so that we can say like the Pharisee, "God, I thank thee, that I am not as other men are, extortioners, unjust, adulterers, or even as this publican" (verse 11).

However, we all should be like the publican, who, "standing afar off, would not lift up so much as his eyes unto heaven, but smote upon his breast, saying, God be merciful to me a sinner" (verse 13). We all need God's mercy because we are all sinners. All the good works and good deeds in the world cannot and will not change this fact. The only cure for our malady is in the blood of Jesus Christ, which is for sin, as Augustus M. Toplady put it in his song "Rock of Ages," the "double cure." It not only frees us from sin's guilt through forgiveness but also from sin's power by cleansing.

When we come to grips with the wretched condition of our desperately wicked and deceitful hearts, we will stop asking why it's necessary to surrender daily, and begin to take up our cross because we understand that this is the only way we can follow Jesus. But let me take a moment to discuss how we became slaves to sin. This will bring into even clearer focus the necessity of total surrender.

In the beginning we were made in God's image and likeness: "And God said, Let us make man in our image, after our likeness: and let them have dominion over the fish of the sea, and over the fowl of the air, and over the cattle, and over all the earth, and over every creeping thing that creepeth upon the earth. So God created man in his own image, in the image of God created he him; male and female created he them" (Gen. 1: 26, 27).

We believe, contrary to the teachings of evolutionists, that we did not come from a lower life form and slowly—over a period of time—evolve to a higher life form. According to the Bible, we came from the hand of One who *is* life. We were made in His image but have since then fallen to our present sinful state. At Creation it was natural for us to do the right thing. When given a choice between right and wrong, we were naturally pulled from within to do right. We received our highest joy in doing God's will, because His laws were written on our hearts.

We were created in such a way that God naturally held first place in our lives. Our love for Him was supreme. Self was lost sight of in our desire to please Him in everything. His will, as expressed in His law, not only controlled our actions but also our every thought. Adam and Eve naturally desired to do God's will, and God's will naturally satisfied their desires. They were always in tune with each other.

This is the way we were created in the beginning, and as long as we were united with God through total surrender, we had perfect peace and happiness. But something happened that disturbed this unity. Do you know what that something was? If you're thinking it was the act of eating the forbidden fruit that disturbed this unity, you're wrong. It wasn't the act itself, but the *choice* to eat of the forbidden fruit that disturbed this unity. As long as Adam and Eve chose to be surrendered to God's will, they continued to have the perfect peace and joy this union brings. This choice is part of bearing the image of God.

God could have made us like robots, with no choice but to do His will. He could have made us like the animals, which live by instinct but have less control over their behavior than we do. God could have made people like slaves, with the ability to choose but not the freedom to exercise it. But Genesis 1:26 says: "And God said, Let us make man in our image, after our likeness."

To bear God's image means that we aren't like robots, mindlessly doing God's will. We aren't like animals, doing God's will instinctively. Neither are we like slaves, doing God's will because we don't have the freedom to choose to do anything else. To be made in His image means that we were not only created with the facility of choice but also with the power and freedom to exercise that choice in reference to God's will.

This freedom of choice was revealed through the presence of the tree of knowledge of good and evil. When God put it in the Garden of Eden, He said: "Of every tree of the garden thou mayest freely eat: but of the tree of the knowledge of good and evil, thou shalt not eat of it: for in the day that thou eatest thereof thou shalt surely die" (Gen. 2:16, 17).

God's purpose in putting this tree in the garden was not to tempt us, because "God cannot be tempted with evil, neither tempteth he any man" (James 1:13). Neither was it God's purpose to limit our freedom, because we were free to eat "of every tree of the garden" except this one. God's purpose in putting this tree in the garden was to enhance Adam's and Eve's power of choice.

How they would choose to exercise this freedom would decide their destiny. They could choose to continue to surrender their wills to God, and by so doing they would continue to enjoy the peace and happiness that comes from this union. Or they could choose not to surrender their wills to God. But to choose the latter would break the union between them and God, who is the only source of life, thereby resulting in death. This is what God told them: "But of the tree of the knowledge of good and evil, thou shalt not eat of it: for in the day that thou eatest thereof thou shalt surely die" (Gen. 2:17).

Though there are many aspects that could be brought out now, I will deal only with what gives us the best insight into what the basis of every sin is, and why we are so hopelessly given to it.

God said that Adam and Eve could eat from every tree in the garden except the tree of knowledge of good and evil, but if they ate from that tree, the result would be death. Notice what Satan, through the serpent, said to Eve: "And the serpent said unto the woman, Ye shall not surely die. For God doth know that in the day ye eat thereof, then your eyes shall be opened, and ye shall be as gods, knowing good and evil" (Gen. 3:4, 5).

Eve now had to make a choice whether to believe what God said or what the serpent said. When God put the tree of knowledge of good and evil in the garden and told Adam and Eve not to eat from it, He was telling them that He was the source of life, joy, peace, and every other good and perfect gift. As long as they believed that and chose to depend on Him to supply these needs, they would have them. But if they chose not to believe Him and decided they could fulfill these needs apart from

Him, they could exercise this choice by eating from the forbidden tree.

The command not to eat of that tree signified God's authority. The choice not to eat from that tree was a choice to surrender to His authority over their lives. The choice to eat from that tree was a choice to rebel against that authority. This was a daily choice, and eventually Eve and Adam made the wrong choice. They chose not to surrender to God's authority, and as a result, they lost the very things they sought.

The choice to rebel against God's authority over our lives, instead of surrendering to it, is the basis of every sin. This, in essence, is a choice to be God, because we take His rightful place in our lives. This is just what Satan told Eve: "For God doth know that in the day ye eat thereof, then your eyes shall be opened, and ye shall be as gods" (verse 5).

In the words "ye shall be as gods," we find what Hebrews 12:1 refers to as "the sin which doth so easily beset us."

It does not say "the sins" (plural), but "the sin" (singular). The root of every sin we commit is in our trying to be "as gods." This was Satan's sin in the beginning. When God created him, he was Lucifer the covering cherub. "Thou art the anointed cherub that covereth; and I have set thee so: thou wast upon the holy mountain of God; thou hast walked up and down in the midst of the stones of fire. Thou wast perfect in thy ways from the day that thou wast created, till iniquity was found in thee" (Eze. 28:14, 15).

The Bible says that Satan, who was then Lucifer, was perfect until iniquity was found in him. What was that iniquity? Isaiah 14:12-14 supplies the answer in these words: "How art thou fallen from heaven, O Lucifer, son of the morning! how art thou cut down to the ground, which didst weaken the nations! For thou hast said in thine heart, I will ascend into heaven, I will exalt my throne above the stars of God: I will sit also upon the mount of the congregation, in the sides of the north: I will ascend above the heights of the clouds; I will be like the most High."

Satan's sin was the desire to exalt himself above God, to exalt his will above God's will. He wanted to be the ultimate authority in his life instead of surrendering to God's authority over his life. Satan desired to take the place of God in his life. As a result, he lost the high position God had given him.

He used the same lie that precipitated his fall to cause Adam and Eve to fall. Since then all humans seem to have been born with the desire to "be as gods." We are born with rebellious hearts. Our minds are at odds with God's law in its natural state. This is why the Martyr struggles with the daily lift and the Happy Christian rejects it. "Because the carnal mind is enmity against God: for it is not subject to the law of God, neither indeed can be. So then they that are in the flesh cannot please God" (Rom. 8:7, 8).

Both the Martyr and the Happy Christian live life in the flesh because neither has chosen to surrender all to Jesus daily. In this state, they can never please God. First Corinthians 2:14 tells us why: "But the natural man receiveth not the things of the Spirit of God: for they are foolishness unto him: neither can he know them, because they are spiritually discerned." So the cross is necessary, because in our natural state we cannot receive the things of God. We may be doing many *good* things, like the rich young ruler, but we do not have eternal life. Eternal life comes with the choice to surrender to God's authority over our lives.

You may feel that you have already surrendered and therefore this doesn't apply to you, but if you didn't surrender today—and throughout the day—you have rejected God's authority and are living in the flesh. Ellen G. White clearly brings out this fact: "There were many in Christ's day, as there are today, over whom the control of Satan for a time seemed broken; through the grace of God they were set free from the evil spirits that had held dominion over the soul. They rejoiced in the love of God; but, like the stony-ground hearers of the parable, they did not abide in His love. They did not surrender themselves to God daily" *(The Desire of Ages,* pp. 323, 324).

Yesterday's choice to surrender isn't good enough. We must take up the cross daily if we are to follow Jesus each day. Throughout all the days prior to their choice to rebel, Adam and Eve had made the choice to surrender, but when they chose to rebel, their previous surrender didn't count.

You may say, "I may not choose to surrender every day, but I never choose to rebel." Well, here's a statement worth pondering: "It is not necessary for us deliberately to choose the service of the kingdom of darkness in order to come under its dominion. We have only to neglect to ally ourselves with the kingdom of light. If we do not co-operate with the heavenly agencies, Satan will take possession of the heart, and will make it his abiding place. The only defense against evil is the indwelling of Christ in the heart through faith in His righteousness. Unless we become vitally connected with God, we can never resist the unhallowed effects of self-love, self-indulgence, and temptation to sin" *(ibid.,* p. 324).

This means that if we don't consciously make the choice to surrender to the Lord daily, we have made the choice to rebel, because Satan will take control of us and make us his slaves. This may be why Jesus said: "He that is not with me is against me" (Matt. 12:30).

There's no middle ground. The choice that Joshua put before the professed followers of God was: "Choose you this day whom ye will serve" (Joshua 24:15). This is the choice we must make every moment of every day of our lives. Have you consciously made your choice today?

Now that we know what the cross experience is and why it is necessary, we need to look at the fears we have that keep us from surrendering daily.

Discussion Questions

1. What truth about ourselves is hard for us to face? (pp. 26, 27)
2. What is the only cure for our sinfulness? (p. 27)
3. In whose image were we created? (p. 28)
4. What did God give us at Creation that distinguishes us from the animal creation? (pp. 28, 29)
5. What was God's purpose in putting the tree of knowledge of good and evil in the garden of Eden? (p. 29)
6. What is the basis of every sin that is committed? Why? (p. 31)
7. What was the iniquity that was found in Lucifer? (pp. 31, 32)
8. Why is it that both the Martyr and the Happy Christian struggle with their daily lift? (p. 32)
9. What does it mean to be "in the flesh"? (pp. 32, 33)
10. Is it possible to be truly surrendered to the Lord one day and not be surrendered the next? If so, how? (p. 33)
11. Is it necessary to choose to rebel against the Lord in order to be in a rebellious state? Why? (p. 33)
12. Does the daily lift mean that I must consciously choose to surrender control of my life to the Lord every day? Why? (pp. 33, 34)

Chapter Three

Our Three Greatest Fears

There is no fear in love; but perfect love casteth out fear: because fear hath torment. He that feareth is not made perfect in love (I John 4:18).

We often shake our heads in disbelief when we read in Genesis 3:1-6 how Eve fell for the serpent's line. We even put on the boots of prejudgment and righteously stomp our feet in anger at her foolishness in believing Satan's lie instead of God's word. We say to ourselves that we would not have done what she did if we had been in her place. This lie even makes us feel that God hasn't dealt fairly with us, and we ask ourselves Why should I have to suffer because of Adam's and Eve's choices?

But, as I said, this is a lie, and we need to stop repeating it, because we continue to do every day the very same thing they did. We suffer as we do, not because of Adam's and Eve's choices, but because of our own choice. Jesus says: "Come unto me, all ye that labour and are heavy laden, and I will give you rest. Take my yoke upon you, and learn of me, for I am meek and lowly in heart: and ye shall find rest unto your souls. For my yoke is easy, and my burden is light" (Matt. 11:28-30).

"Those who take Christ at His word, and surrender their souls to His keeping, their lives to His ordering, will find peace and quietude. Nothing of the world can make them sad when Jesus makes them glad by His presence. In perfect acquiescence there is perfect rest" *(The Desire of Ages,* p. 331).

The word "acquiescence" means to yield or to agree with apart from protest. When we yield perfectly to the Lord's will for our lives, without protest or complaint, we will find perfect peace. Nothing in this world will be able to disturb it. This is the sure result of surrender. We suffer so much heartache and pain because we choose not to surrender or we neglect to surrender ourselves and our desires to the Lord. Now, most of us already know that the Lord promises peace if we come to Him in humble submissiveness, but why is it we don't do it?

"But many who profess to be His followers have an anxious, troubled heart, because they are afraid to trust themselves with God. . . . Unless they do make this surrender, they cannot find peace" *(ibid.,* p. 330).

We do not make the choice to surrender because we are *afraid* to trust God. This is exactly why Adam and Eve chose not to surrender. They, too, were afraid to trust themselves with God. But why are we afraid of God? Is there any good reason? The answer to that question is no, there is no *good* reason. But there is a reason. It's the same reason that Eve was afraid to trust Him. The reason is that we, like Eve, too often believe the lies Satan tells us about God, instead of believing what God says about Himself in His Word.

These lies are brought out in Genesis 3:1-5. In essence, Satan says that if you surrender to God's authority, you will (1) miss out on a better and happier existence ("your eyes shall be opened" [verse 5]); (2) not be in control of your life ("ye shall be as gods" [verse 5]); and (3) limit your personal growth ("you shall not eat of every tree?" [verse 1]). These lies make us afraid to trust God, and this makes surrender impossible.

Whenever we find ourselves struggling with surrender to God's will, whenever we find it hard to obey His Word, it's because one or more of these fears is the focus of our conscious or subconscious thinking. Instead of gritting our teeth and trying hard to do the right thing, which is what the Martyr does, we first need to deal with the lie that makes us afraid.

I have not always understood this, and this lack of understanding caused me to struggle with my daily lift many times. Some days I would leave my cross lying on the ground. I didn't leave it on the ground because I was trying to be rebellious or because I didn't want to do right. No, I left it because I hadn't faced my fear or fears in a specific manner. First John 4:18 tells us that before we can follow the Lord to perfection, we must cast out the fears that torment us. It also lets us know that perfect love is what casts out the fear.

Of course, this text cannot be speaking of *our* perfect love, because "there is no fear in love." It is God's perfect love for us that is referred to here. As our faith grasps the truths of God's Word, we begin to understand how perfectly God loves us. This understanding begins to generate a love within us for Him. The more we learn of God's perfect love for us, through the study of His Word, the more we come to love and trust Him. The more we love and trust God, the less fearful we are of surrendering to His control. The more we surrender to God's control, the more like Him (the more perfect) we become. This is how we are "made perfect in love" (1 John 4:18).

"Christian workers who succeed in their efforts must know Christ; and in order to know Him, they must know His love. . . . This redeeming power, filling the heart, would control every other motive and raise its possessors above the corrupting influences of the world. And as this love was allowed full sway and became the motive power in the life, their trust and confidence in God and His dealing with them would be complete" *(The Acts of the Apostles*, pp. 551, 552).

The rest of this chapter will discuss the three major fears that keep us from surrender. I will apply the truth of God's Word to each one and expose Satan's lie. If that lie has been making you fearful of taking up your cross daily and following Jesus, you'll be set free from its paralyzing grip as you choose to believe God's Word instead of Satan's lie.

The Fear of Missing Out on a Better and Happier Life

In essence, this fear is based on the belief that we will not be happy with what God wants to do *for* us, *with* us, and *in* us. By that I don't mean to imply that we think God's will is not good. Most of us believe that God's will is always good. We may even believe that His will is good for us. What we sometimes doubt is whether God's will is good *to* us.

The fear that we will not be better off and happier with God's will has a multitude of related fears, such as the fear of failure, fear of loss, fear of rejection, and many others, all of which make us afraid to surrender to Him. Whenever we are struggling with surrender, this fear is involved in one way or another. That's why I decided to deal with this fear first.

There are times when God's will is so radically opposed to all that seems right to our natural senses that surrendering self seems to be the most outrageous thing to do. It seems to violate the essence of not only who we are but all that we stand for. At those times, every natural impulse in us recoils from lifting the cross of surrender. We are convinced that if we did what God requires of us, we would be absolutely miserable.

These are the times when surrender to God is the

hardest thing in the world to do. We would rather be told to do some good thing, no matter how hard it may be or how much material sacrifice it calls for, as long as we do not have to surrender to God's will on that issue. But if we are to enter the joy of the Lord, surrender we must. Anything short of this is walking in the flesh, and no matter how good our lives may be, we aren't pleasing God if we're walking in the flesh. The only way to find true peace with ourselves and to please God as well is to allow God's love to cast out the fear.

Let me share with you one of the times when I struggled with my daily lift because I believed this lie and how I had to allow God's love to cast out my fear before I could continue to follow Him.

When I first gave my heart to Jesus, I had a lot of blatantly sinful habits. Blatant because some of us have problems with more socially acceptable sins, such as a bad temper, holding grudges, and backbiting. These sins are more acceptable to the saints. (Notice I said the saints, not God.) We can hide these kinds of sins under the religious garb of righteous indignation against sin, holy zeal for the Lord, or godly concern for our erring brother or sister.

But the sins that I came to the Lord with were too wolfish to hide under such sheep's clothing. They had to go. Two of these were addiction to heroin (I was a junkie for more than three years) and cigarettes (I smoked for more than 10 years, and when I stopped, I was smoking at least two packs a day).

When I surrendered my life to Jesus and confessed Him as not only my Saviour but also my Lord, I got immediate victory over these sins. I had tried many times before to stop smoking and drugging on my own, only to find that I was a hopeless slave to them both mentally and physically. I had started doing drugs and smoking under the false illusion of being free to do my own thing, only to end up a slave and totally dominated by Satan through these sinful habits.

I grew to hate the control these sins had over my life (not to mention the other sins that these led to). I longed to be set free from them. After trying everything I knew to overcome them (including substituting other drugs), I finally came to grips with the truth that I was powerless to save myself. I realized, like Paul, that "in me . . . dwelleth no good thing" (Rom. 7:18). This is when my religious upbringing proved invaluable, because it offered me hope in a time of utter hopelessness.

I was reared in a Christian home by a sincere Christian mother who sacrificed many worldly comforts to give me a Christian education (I attended Dupont Park Seventh-day Adventist School in Washington, D.C., grades 1-10, and graduated from Takoma Academy, Takoma Park, Maryland, in 1967). For a long time it seemed that my mother had made these sacrifices for nothing, but she never gave up praying for and believing in me. Finally, all the sacrifices she'd made in order for me to have a Christian education and the many hours spent in praying for me to come to my senses and give my life to the Lord paid off.

Some of my friends had come to that turning point in their lives, but they were unable to make the transition from death to life because they didn't have any godly background from which to draw. The tremendous fear that one experiences when contemplating the gigantic step of faith across the seemingly endless chasm that stretches between the old life of sin and the new life of righteousness in Christ overwhelmed them and held them captive. For them, as for many others, the chasm was too wide—the gulf was fixed.

But when I reached this point, I had something upon which to draw that compelled me to move forward. I too was gripped with the feeling of fear and apprehension, but I also felt the power of my mother's many prayers. My ears echoed with the stories of God's love, forgiveness, and acceptance that I had not only learned from my grandfather but had also heard in church school, Sabbath school, and Sabbath sermons (though I slept, talked, and played through many of them).

These all proved an invaluable help to me when I, like the prodigal son, "came to myself." They gave me the courage to "arise and go" to my heavenly Father with the confidence that He would meet me while I was a "great way off" and cover my wretchedness with His robe of righteousness. I will go more into how I made this transition in the next chapter. Suffice it to say, I gave my life to the Lord. From that day in October 1973 to this present time, I haven't even had a desire to do any more drugs or smoke another cigarette or joint (marijuana).

Before you get too carried away with praising the Lord for my deliverance from heroin and nicotine addiction, I must confess that I started drinking. Even though the Lord had delivered me from my heroin and smoking addictions, I drank at least a pint of gin a day. This went on for about two months.

Why do you suppose I did that? Some may say I wasn't converted, or I wasn't sincere enough, or I was baptized too soon, or I was a hypocrite, or I didn't exercise enough willpower. But none of these was my real problem. My problem wasn't lack of sincerity or willpower, or any of the other reasons we usually attribute to struggling Christians. My problem was *fear,* and that fear kept me from surrendering.

You see, I was sick and tired of my addiction to drugs and smoking. I was convinced that I would have a better and happier life without them. This made it easy for me to surrender to God's authority concerning the use of them. As I did my part, which is surrender, He did His part. John 1:12 tells us what His part is: "But as many as received him, to them gave he power to become the sons of God, even to them that believe on his name."

The moment I confessed Jesus as Lord and Saviour of my life, my faith was able to grab hold of His power to overcome those sins that had held me captive for years. I experienced immediate victory. This is why I know there's nothing too hard for God. He can give us immediate victory over any sin if we want it with all our heart. However, here's where I faltered. Whereas I wanted freedom from heroin and nicotine with all my heart, I didn't want freedom from *all* drugs with *all* my heart.

In Jeremiah 29:13 the Lord says: "And ye shall seek me, and find me, when ye shall search for me with all your heart." I did not search for God with all my heart on the drinking issue because I was believing one of Satan's lies.

You see, the moment Jesus set me free from cigarettes and heroin, the devil got upset, scared, and busy. He began to fabricate a lie just for me. His lie was based on the premise that I would not be happy if I gave the Lord total control of that area of my life. He suggested that since I'd been dependent on drugs for so long, living a drug-free life wouldn't make me happy. Therefore, I would need some kind of substance, just for a little while, to keep myself together. I wouldn't use those same substances, because I couldn't handle them, but I permitted myself to be deceived into thinking that a little alcohol wouldn't hurt. After all, God would understand. He didn't expect me just to quit everything cold turkey. Armed with this lie, I began drinking daily, and my drinking got totally out of control.

You cannot tell me that God isn't longsuffering and kind. He allowed me to go on like that for at least two months without allowing the saints at the church that I had just joined to find out. He didn't do this because He condoned my sin. He did it because He knew my sin wasn't one of rebellion, but rather of ignorance. I don't mean to imply that I didn't know drinking was wrong, because I did. But what I didn't fully know was how good and loving and kind God is and that He would make me far happier than any substance I might ingest if I'd just choose to depend fully on Him.

He realized that once He brought me to a deeper understanding of His loving character, it would awaken a greater love for Him in my heart. That love would then cast out the fear that had kept me from surrendering this area of my life to His loving control.

God accomplished this by exposing the lie I'd been believing. He let me see that my drinking made me a worse slave than the other two addictions put together. I can remember the day the Holy Spirit brought that conviction to me. I was sitting on the side of my bed, feeling bad about how I was hurting my wife, who was pregnant with our first son. (We now have three handsome sons—Gregory, Jr., Michael, and Eric.) I was also destroying my life with the alcohol. This realization made me want to drink more in the hope of finding some momentary peace of mind.

As I was lifting the bottle to my lips, the Lord, through the power of the Holy Spirit, spoke to my mind in these words: "Greg, you'll never find the peace and happiness you want until you stop depending on that bottle and start depending on Me, and Me alone. Greg, it's either Me or that bottle. Choose you this day whom you will serve."

At that moment, the fear of losing the joy of the Lord cast out the lie that Satan had used to bind me, and I cried out, "Lord, I choose You." At that very moment I was set free from my slavery to alcohol. I now believe the truth expressed in John 10:10: "The thief cometh not, but for to steal, and to kill, and to destroy: I am come that they might have life, and that they might have it more abundantly."

I'd been listening to the lies of the thief, and he was stealing my joy, killing me with alcohol, and destroying my family. He had me convinced that Jesus was the thief. I don't mean I actually came out and said that. I didn't even realize at the time that I was thinking that way. If someone had told me this was what I was doing, I would have vehemently denied it. But the fact is, I did believe that if I surrendered to the Lord's control on this issue I wouldn't be happy. I thought Jesus would steal my joy and make my life miserable.

Some of you have seen Jesus as the thief. Whenever you struggle with surrender of anything in your life, it's because you're afraid He will make you unhappy. But I want you to know that Jesus loves you more than you love yourself. Don't be afraid to trust Him with *everything.* He means it when He says He has come to give us the abundant life.

Whenever I find myself struggling with my daily lift, I tell myself the truth. And the truth is that the only way to a better and happier existence is the way of the cross, which brings me to fear number 2.

The Fear of Losing Control Over Our Lives

Another fear that we have is based on the lie that if we give the Lord total control, we'll lose control over our lives. We worry that we'll become spiritual zombies, who have no minds and no wills because God has taken over. This is why some sincere Christians fight the concept of giving God total control. They're afraid that this violates the free will that the Lord has given them to exercise and reduces them to being mere robots or spiritual clones.

But nothing could be further from the truth. This is just a different version of the same lie that Satan told Eve when he said that she would "be as gods" if she rebelled against God's authority over her life. Of course, we can clearly see Eve's foolishness when she fell for this lie. But we suddenly go blind when it comes to seeing how we fall for the same lie.

Jesus gave us the real truth when He said: "He that findeth his life shall lose it: and he that loseth his life for my sake shall find it" (Matt. 10:39).

According to Satan's lie, to find our lives is to choose to be in control, instead of surrendering that control to the Lord. The truth is, when we do that, we lose the very thing we seek—as did Eve. It's only when we choose to surrender that control to the Lord that we find the thing we desire, even though we didn't seek it. This is because God made us. He has given us all the desires we have, and He alone can satisfy them. This He has promised to do as long as we are surrendered to His control. God's Word says: "Delight thyself also in the Lord; and he shall give thee the desires of thine heart" (Ps. 37:4).

According to *Strong's Exhaustive Concordance of the Bible,* the Hebrew word for delight here is *anag.* It can mean being delicate or soft or pliable, thus denoting submissiveness. The psalmist is saying that if we are soft and pliable in the Lord's hands, allowing Him to mold and shape us in accordance with His will, He will give us the very things our hearts desire.

There's no basic desire we have that's sinful in and of itself. What makes a desire sinful is the way in which we seek to satisfy it. When we seek to satisfy our desires in a way that's not in accordance with the Lord's will, then they are sinful desires. But when we take those same desires to the Lord in a submissive attitude, we can rest assured that we'll have whatever it is we desire.

Martyr Christian, I have good news for you. You can have the desires of your heart satisfied while here on this earth. But, Happy Christian, it isn't always in the way that you are seeking to satisfy your desires, because our desperately wicked and deceitful hearts cannot always be trusted to ask for satisfaction of these desires in the right way. So we must be willing to let the Lord answer our prayers anyway He sees fit.

This is what it means to delight yourself in the Lord. You can do this because you believe His way will satisfy your desires far better than any way you could devise. Paul's testimony is: "Now unto him that is able to do exceeding abundantly above all that we ask or think, according to the power that worketh in us" (Eph. 3:20).

So the only way to get the control over our lives that we truly desire is to stop seeking to get it and start surrendering more fully to the Lord. When we do this, the Lord will begin to restore us to the status we had when He created us. Genesis 1:28 tells us what that status was: "And God blessed them, and God said unto them, Be fruitful, and multiply, and replenish the earth, and subdue it: and have dominion over the fish of the sea, and over the fowl of the air, and over every living thing that moveth upon the earth."

The word "dominion" means treading down, subjugating, rule, or reign. God's original intention for human beings was that we would have dominion over everything in this world, reigning and ruling over it. He intended that everything animate and inanimate, large and small, would be under human control. *Homo sapiens,* like God, were to have a kingdom over which to reign—a kingdom that reached from the fowls that flew in the heaven, to the fish that swam in the depths of the sea, and to everything in between. As long as humanity would choose to stay under God's authority, He would give it control over everything on this earth.

Adam and Eve enjoyed this control until Eve fell for

Satan's lie that she wasn't really in control of her life or her environment as long as she was under God's authority. Satan suggested that she be as God, who did not submit His will to anyone. Therefore she would have to defy His authority and assert her own will in order to be in total control of her life.

This lie sounded logical to Eve, so she ate the forbidden fruit. She then gave some to Adam, who also ate of the fruit. It was only then that "the eyes of them both were opened," and they realized that they had fallen for a lie. But it was too late. Satan had beguiled them into surrendering their God-given control to him. He now had the dominion God had originally given to them. They lost control by seeking to get control. If they had chosen to believe the word of the Lord instead of their feelings at the time, they wouldn't have been deceived.

God realized that Adam's and Eve's choices came from a lack of understanding His loving character, so He put into operation the plan He had prepared as a remedy for this situation. This plan would make it possible for fallen humanity to be restored to its original status. Had this plan not been in place prior to Adam's and Eve's choosing to sin, they would have died the moment they disobeyed God and ate the forbidden fruit. This is why Jesus is called "the Lamb slain from the foundation of the world" (Rev. 13:8).

When this plan is referred to in the Bible, it is preceded by the word "mystery," such as the "mystery of the kingdom of God" (Mark 4:11), the "mystery of the gospel" (Eph. 6:19), the "mystery of Christ" (Eph. 3:4), and the "mystery of God" (Rev. 10:7). It's called a mystery because God didn't reveal it until after Adam's and Eve's fall, and even then He didn't reveal all the details. God chose to unfold this mystery not only to mankind but also to the whole universe more and more as time went on, until it would be fully revealed or finished.

So in Genesis, the first book of the Bible, we see the beginning of the unfolding of this mystery as we read the promise that God gave Adam and Eve after they had come under Satan's control: "And I will put enmity between thee and the woman, and between thy seed and her seed; it shall bruise thy head, and thou shalt bruise his heel" (Gen. 3:15).

In Revelation, the last book of the Bible, we find out when this mystery will be finished: "But in the days of the voice of the seventh angel, when he shall begin to sound, the mystery of God should be finished, as he hath declared to his servants the prophets" (Rev. 10:7).

But it is in between these two books that God reveals what the "mystery" truly is: "And without controversy great is the mystery of godliness: God was manifest in the flesh, justified in the Spirit, seen of angels, preached unto the Gentiles, believed on in the world, received up into glory" (1 Tim. 3:16).

We see here that the mystery was that God the Son—the preincarnate Christ—would humble Himself and become one of us, overcome sin in the flesh, and die on the cross for our sins. This was truly a mystery to the angelic host as well as the entire universe. That God, the Creator of everything, would condescend to become a human being, humble Himself, and become obedient unto death, especially the shameful death of the cross, was beyond comprehension.

But the mystery does not end there. It says that Jesus was "received up into glory." This brings out another phase of the unfolding of the mystery. The book of Hebrews explains this phase in detail. In essence, it lets us know that Jesus is our high priest now in the heavenly sanctuary. Hebrews 8 tells us it is because of this that we can now enter into the "new covenant" relationship. And the result is revealed in Colossians 1:26-28: "Even the mystery which hath been hid from ages and from generations, but now is made manifest to his saints: to whom God would make known what is the riches of the glory of this mystery among the Gentiles; which is Christ in you, the hope of glory: whom we preach, warning every man, and teaching every man in wisdom; that we may present every man perfect in Christ Jesus."

The mystery that God is revealing is more than the fact that Jesus could live in the flesh and not sin. The greater mystery is that Jesus can live in my flesh and keep me from sinning. Jude 24, 25 says: "Now unto him that is able to keep you from falling, and to present you faultless before the presence of his glory with exceeding joy, to the only wise God our Saviour, be glory and majesty, dominion and power, both now and ever. Amen."

The fact that God can take sinful human beings and restore them to this original status, which is in "His Image," reveals to the universe God's wisdom, glory, majesty, dominion, and power. This is the high and holy calling of everyone who claims to be a follower of Jesus Christ. This is the mystery that will be finished, and it's the privilege of the church to reflect God's image fully to the universe.

This is how Paul states this truth: "And to make all men see what is the fellowship of the mystery, which from the beginning of the world hath been hid in God, who created all things by Jesus Christ: to the intent that now unto the principalities and powers in heavenly places might be known by the church the manifold wisdom of God, according to the eternal purpose which he purposed in Christ Jesus our Lord" (Eph. 3:9-11).

All this was truly a mystery to me at one time—a mystery that I once found very hard to comprehend. I just couldn't see how God, through Jesus, could keep me from sinning. I had tried to get the victory over certain sins in my life, only to fail again and again. I had just about given up on the hope of total restoration from sin. I had begun to believe that the Lord couldn't keep me from falling, and if He was going to save me, He'd have to save me in sin.

The Lord delivered me from Satan's lie by giving me a correct understanding of what it meant to lift my cross daily. Then I began to understand that Jesus could keep me from sinning. The hope of living a victorious life returned. I discovered that the same power that kept Jesus from sin is able to keep me from sinning also as I surrender control of my life to Him. I found that as I gave Jesus control, He gave me strength to be in control. "The greatest triumph given us by the religion of Christ is control over ourselves" (*Testimonies*, vol. 4, p. 235).

Satan had bound me with the fear of losing control over my life, but now I have been set free by the truth that through surrender to Jesus I gain control over my life.

Since I have learned the true meaning of the cross and have begun lifting it daily, the Lord has been giving me more and more victory and more and more self-control. Sins that I once thought I could never overcome or ever even want to overcome, through the power of Jesus Christ, are being put away, and I don't even miss them! Don't get me wrong, by no means do I want you to get the idea that I think I've arrived, because I haven't. But, like Paul, "this one thing I do, forgetting those things which are behind, and reaching forth unto those things which are before, I press toward the mark for the prize of the high calling of God in Christ Jesus" (Phil. 3:13, 14).

We now go on to face our third greatest fear.

Fear of Limiting Our Personal Growth

Today we hear much talk about self-actualization or

the development of self to the point that self has been exalted to the position of a god. This so-called New Age thinking has not only dominated secular thought, but also it has made its way into the religious world.

The concept of "sin" has become outdated and outmoded. To this "enlightened" way of thinking, there is no sin, only what's right or wrong for an individual. God's law is no longer the standard of righteousness. What determines that which is right for one's emotional and physical well-being is whatever happens to be best as perceived by that individual, thus making self the ultimate authority.

All this is made legitimate by saying that one must first get in touch with the God in oneself. Of course, God's Word lets us know that in our natural state there is no God in us: "As it is written, There is none righteous, no, not one" (Rom. 3:10). It also says: "There is a way which seemeth right unto a man, but the end thereof are the ways of death" (Prov. 14:12).

This is because "the heart is deceitful above all things, and desperately wicked: who can know it?" (Jer. 17:9). Therefore we are told to "trust in the Lord with all thine heart; and lean not unto thine own understanding. In all thy ways acknowledge him, and he shall direct thy paths" (Prov. 3:5, 6).

The New Age movement is based on an updated version of the same old lie that Satan used to deceive Eve. By using the serpent as his tool in the garden of Eden, he told her that God's law forbidding her to eat from the tree of knowledge of good and evil was limiting her personal development and that if she ate from it, she would become more enlightened. This implied that God's authority was keeping her from experiencing personal growth. So we read: "And when the woman saw that the tree was good for food, and that it was pleasant to the eyes, and a tree to be desired to make one wise, she took of the fruit thereof, and did eat" (Gen. 3:6).

That lie still sounds good today. But the end thereof is still death.

You may be saying to yourself that you don't believe in that new stuff—be it New Age or new theology. No sir, you practice that old-time religion—the kind that Paul and Silas preached—and you're not afraid to call sin by its right name. Well, I hope that's true, but if you've found yourself struggling from time to time with surrender, it may be because you have, to some degree, bought into Satan's old lie dressed up in this new way.

I must confess that I've been deceived by this old lie. I don't mean that I adhere to the new stuff, but it really doesn't matter to Satan whether I fall for the old or new version. I'm his slave either way because I'm afraid to find freedom in the cross.

Being sinful by nature, we all have a natural desire to exalt self to the status of God. This is what makes daily surrender necessary, but it is also what makes it a very scary thing. The thought of it sends cold chills down one's spine because we all have dreams and aspirations that we want to realize. We have goals we long to reach, but we hear in the call to take up the cross daily Jesus' voice saying, "You must relinquish control of those cherished dreams and goals and surrender to My will and timetable for your life." His call makes us fearful that we'll never reach our fullest potential or live out our dreams.

I can remember how I struggled with this fear, which in turn caused me to struggle with surrendering daily. I had always believed in the concept of daily surrender, but I didn't fully understand it or know how to do it until a dear friend of mine lent me her tapes on *The Sanctuary,* by Carol Zarska. Before this happened, I had been a sincere Christian pastor, serving the Lord to the best of my knowledge. I had been surrendering to God the best way I knew how and always thinking it was total. However, I knew that something was missing, but I didn't know just what it was. As I sought the Lord for more wisdom, He brought me to these tapes. A whole new world of truth opened up to me. I don't mean new light. I mean, rather, that old truths began to shine brightly with new meaning.

I knew the historical teachings of the sanctuary truth that we as Seventh-day Adventists learn in our schools, but I didn't know it as *present truth.* It was truth to me, but it wasn't specifically applicable to the time in which I was living. As God spoke to me through these tapes, I came to understand what the psalmist meant when he said: "Thy way, O God, is in the sanctuary" (Ps. 77:13).

My newfound understanding of the sanctuary truth taught me the way to have a more intimate walk with the Lord, because it showed me the steps to take in the process of surrender through prayer. My prayer life became more fervent and effective. My study of God's Word was more of a reality. The Lord began to reveal my sins to me on a much deeper level. He showed me the secret thoughts and intents of my sinful heart, and as I surrendered to His leading, He not only forgave me but also cleansed my life of their defiling influence.

But eventually I hit a snag and began to miss the intimacy with the Lord that I had come to enjoy so much. I still got up early every morning and communed with the Lord through prayer and Bible study, but I didn't feel His presence as powerfully as in previous times. This greatly disturbed me, and I began to ask the Lord to show me the problem. This went on for a while until one day while talking to a doctor friend of mine, the Lord revealed the problem to me. In the past, God had used me to bless my friend, but this day God used him to bless me.

As I shared my concern with him he said, "Whenever that happens to me, it's always because there's some area in my that life God wants me to surrender to Him, and I'm holding back."

At that moment the Lord spoke to me, saying, "Greg, you're afraid to give Me total control of your ministry." The Lord had been trying to show me this, but I had fought it because I was afraid to face the truth. The Lord knew I needed help in coming to grips with my fear, so He sent a friend to give me courage. Little did my friend know how much he blessed me that day. When he left, I got down on my knees and gave the Lord *complete* control of my ministry.

I had been surrendering more and more of my life to the Lord. As my walk with Him grew more intimate, His light of truth shone brighter and went deeper, revealing that the areas I had already surrendered needed to be surrendered on an even deeper level. At each level I reached, I surrendered until He began to deal with my ministry.

As I said earlier, I had already surrendered this area of my life to the Lord, but that surrender was based on the knowledge I had of the Lord at that time. I had grown comfortable with this level of surrender. As I measured my commitment to the Lord by that of some of my brothers and sisters, I told myself that I had given the Lord total control of my ministry. Consciously I fully believed I had. But deep down in my subconscious mind lurked the crippling fear that if I gave the Lord total control of my ministry, I'd never realize some of the goals and aspirations I had set for myself. I feared that I'd never become the me I longed to be.

You see, I take my ministry very seriously. It's not just a job or even a way of life. It *is* my life. I put my all into it. This might even seem to be how the Lord would want it to be, because this attitude made me dedicated. But this dedication was to self—not to God. Don't misunderstand me, it wasn't that I was not sincerely trying to serve the Lord. It was just that I didn't realize I was trying to serve two masters at the same time—the Lord and self.

When I prayed for the Lord to give me a sermon for His people (which I always do), I not only wanted that sermon to be a spiritual blessing to the congregation, but I also wanted it to make me look good so that I'd be known as a powerful preacher. This meant that when God wanted me to preach a sermon that wouldn't make the saints feel like they had a high day in Zion, I had to struggle with preaching it. Sometimes I would grit my teeth and say, "I'm going to let the Lord use me," but self would always get in the way. Even when I preached the sermon, I'd sometimes convince myself it wasn't the right message.

I'd depend on the Lord for guidance and strength, but all too often I limited that guidance and strength to fit my personal ambitions and goals. This was easy for me to do because my ambitions and goals were based on spiritual things. I didn't want a lot of money and worldly fame. I just wanted to be a powerful preacher and a productive soul winner. Little did I realize that this was my way of wanting to be popular and famous. I too wanted my praises to be sung, only I wanted mine sung to the tune of "Jesus, Keep Me Near the Cross" instead of "I Did It My Way." But it doesn't matter what tune you sing; it's still the same sinful self that must be crucified before God can be glorified.

God worked patiently with me, overruling my ignorance so that I wouldn't deprive His people of the blessings He intended them to receive. He was able to do this because of my sincerity. I'm glad that God knew what was in my heart. He knew I just needed the truth to set me free. That's why God was able to use the disciples in their undone state—not because they were worthy and without fault, but because they were sincere and teachable despite their faults. "And the times of this ignorance God winked at; but now commandeth all men to repent" (Acts 17:30).

God had been winking at my ignorance, but now He was shedding light on what had been darkness. Therefore, repentance was in order. I had to make a choice whether to surrender my cherished idol to the Lord or continue to serve it, which was the same as serving myself. For me, this was tantamount to the rich young ruler's giving all his riches to the poor. No wonder I had fought this realization for so long, but now that the Lord had made it clear, I didn't hesitate to give it to Him.

The moment I surrendered, a wave of peace came over me that I cannot describe, and I felt the intimate presence of the Lord return. Each morning I surrender that area of my life to Him anew. As a result, I have more peace, happiness, satisfaction, and power than I've ever had before.

"Christ in His life on earth made no plans for Himself. He accepted God's plans for Him, and day by day the Father unfolded His plans. So should we depend upon God, that our lives may be the simple outworking of His will. As we commit our ways to Him, He will direct our steps. Too many, in planning for a brilliant future, make an utter failure. Let God plan for you. . . . God never leads His children otherwise than they would choose to be led, if they could see the end from the beginning and discern the glory of the purpose which they are fulfilling as coworkers with Him" (Ellen G. White, *The Ministry of Healing*, p. 479).

For many Christians, their careers are their idols. We often view our careers as the best way to develop fully into the kind of person we desire to become. We look to our careers to provide us with the kind of living that we dream of and the prestige that we feel we deserve. We set our own goals and timetables as to when we feel we should be at a certain level, and when the least little thing goes wrong, our peace and happiness leave us. There's much anger—even hatred—in our hearts when we're passed over for a raise or a promotion or when we're not given proper recognition. God forbid that we should be demoted or—worse yet—fired! When this happens, it seems as if our whole world has fallen apart, and it has, because our jobs or careers have become our whole world and have taken God's place. Many times God allows things to go wrong for us in this area of our lives in order for us to see the "unknown god" we serve.

Have you given the Lord total control of your career? Are you seeking His plans for your life daily? Have you surrendered your timetable to the timetable of God's will? Are you struggling with your daily lift in this area of your life? If so, it's because you're still believing Satan's old lie that you'll be limiting your personal growth. Don't continue to fall for that lie.

God made you in His image. The goal He has set for you is higher than the one you have set for yourself. Don't settle for your low standard. Tie into God's ideal for your life. He'll take you higher than your human thoughts can reach. You'll go beyond what you perceive as your potential as a human being because you'll become a partaker of divinity (see 2 Peter 1:4). You'll find that He is able to do "exceeding abundantly" more than you can ask or think (Eph. 3:20).

"The only condition upon which the freedom of man is possible is that of becoming one with Christ. 'The truth shall make you free;' and Christ is the truth. . . . Subjection to God is restoration to one's self—to the true glory and dignity of man" (*The Desire of Ages,* p. 466).

So far we've dealt with what the cross is, why it's necessary, and the three fears that cause us to struggle with surrender. Now we're ready to deal with how to surrender.

Discussion Questions

1. What lie makes us feel that God has dealt unfairly with us? Why is it a lie? (p. 35)
2. What brings perfect peace? (pp. 35, 36)
3. What is the problem when we find it hard to lift our cross? (p. 36)
4. What are the three major lies that cause us to be afraid to surrender all? (p. 36)
5. What must we do with our fears before we can surrender? (p. 37)
6. What is the first fear? Relate how you've struggled with surrender because of this lie. (p. 38)
7. Can we get immediate victory over our known sins? If so, why do we sometimes struggle with victory? (pp. 39-43)
8. How do we show doubt regarding what Jesus said in John 10:10? (pp. 43-44)
9. What is the second major fear? Relate your struggle because of this fear. (p. 44)
10. What does Matthew 10:39 mean? (p. 45)
11. What does it mean to delight yourself in the Lord? (p. 46)
12. Why must we be willing to let the Lord answer our prayers in the way He sees fit? (p. 46)
13. Will the Lord's way of answering our prayers satisfy us? Why? (p. 46)
14. What did God give to humanity at Creation that was given over to Satan by Adam and Eve? (pp. 46, 47)

15. How did they lose it? (p. 47)

16. What is God's plan to restore that which we lost called? Why? (p. 47)

17. What is the "mystery" that God wants to reveal in us? (pp. 48, 49)

18. How is this "mystery" finished? (pp. 49, 50)

19. What is the third major fear? Relate your struggle because of this fear. (pp. 50, 51)

20. Is it possible for us to be deceived by this lie while not professing a belief in it? If so, how? (pp. 51, 52)

21. In what area of our lives do we show that we've been deceived by this lie? Why? (pp. 56, 57)

22. How should every follower of Christ live as far as his goals and plans are concerned? (p. 56)

23. How can we tell whether we have made an idol of our jobs and careers? (pp. 56, 57)

24. Is God's goal for us higher or lower than our goals for ourselves? How do you know? (p. 57)

25. What is the only way to be restored to our true selves? (pp. 57, 58)

Chapter Four

The How-to of Surrender

I am crucified with Christ: nevertheless I live; yet not I, but Christ liveth in me: and the life which I now live in the flesh I live by the faith of the Son of God, who loved me, and gave himself for me (Gal. 2:20).

One of the most difficult questions to answer is How do I give my will to God? For years I struggled to find the answer to this question until I came to understand this statement found in *Steps to Christ.* It's quite long, but because it's so powerful I'll quote it in its entirety.

"Many are inquiring, '*How* am I to make the surrender of myself to God?' You desire to give yourself to Him, but you are weak in moral power, in slavery to doubt, and controlled by the habits of your life of sin. Your promises and resolutions are like ropes of sand. You cannot control your thoughts, your impulses, your affections. The knowledge of your broken promises and forfeited pledges weakens your confidence in your own sincerity, and causes you to feel that God cannot accept you; but you need not despair. What you need to understand is the true force of the will. This is the governing power in the nature of man, the power of decision, or of choice. Everything depends on the right action of the will. The power of choice God has given to men; it is theirs to exercise. You cannot change your heart, you cannot of yourself give to

God its affections; but you can *choose* to serve Him. You can give Him your will; He will then work in you to will and to do according to His good pleasure. Thus your whole nature will be brought under the control of the Spirit of Christ; your affections will be centered upon Him, your thoughts will be in harmony with Him. . . .

"Many will be lost while hoping and desiring to be Christians. . . . Through the right exercise of the will, an entire change may be made in your life. By yielding up your will to Christ, you ally yourself with the power that is above all principalities and powers" (pp. 47, 48).

The key to the act of surrendering is understanding "the true force of the will" and using it in the right way. Many people think this means willpower, but if you read the condition of the person referred to in the statement, you'll realize this person has no power to his will. So the statement is not talking about willpower as we normally think of it. Let's look at that portion of the statement again and see what it really is saying.

"What you need to understand is the true force of the will. This is the governing power in the nature of man, the power of decision, or of choice." The *"power of decision, or of choice"* is the focus here. When we learn to use it in the right way, an entire change will be brought about in our lives. We'll become new creatures in Jesus Christ. But how are we to use this "power of choice"?

Let's examine what the statement says about that: "You cannot change your heart, you cannot of yourself give to God its affections; but you can *choose* to serve Him. You can give Him your will; He will then work in you to will and to do according to His good pleasure."

The statement points out that the right use of the will is composed of two things: (1) making a choice, or decision, to obey the Lord and (2) surrendering that choice to Jesus, believing He will give you the power to do what you have chosen to do. These two things give the Lord permission to work in you both to will and to do His good pleasure. This is what it means to "give Him your will."

This is why surrendering the will to God is the ultimate freedom. Satan has us bound by sin, and we are born his slaves (Ps. 51:5). We don't realize this until we try to free ourselves from the sinful habits that have dominated our lives and we try to live a righteous life. Then we realize how much of a slave we really are. Paul talks about this in Romans 7. He describes a person who thought he was free until the Lord revealed to him the spiritual meaning of His law (verse 9). He repented of his sins and decided he was going to obey the law, only to find he was a slave to sin (verses 10-20).

In verses 21-24 he comes to this conclusion: "I find then a law, that, when I would do good, evil is present with me. For I delight in the law of God after the inward man: but I see another law in my members, warring against the law of my mind, and bringing me into captivity to the law of sin which is in my members. O wretched man that I am! who shall deliver me from the body of this death?"

The only way of deliverance from a life of sin is through Jesus (verse 25). He has conquered sin and Satan on our behalf. But He respects our choice. He'll never force Himself on us and make us do His will. Rather, that's what Satan does. Jesus will do only what we allow Him to do. He respects our choice. *We must choose to allow Him to do for us what we really desire but do not have the power to accomplish.*

When we learn to stop wishing we could do right or trying to do God's will with our own strength and begin giving to Jesus a firm decision to do whatever He desires of us, we'll then find all the power we need to do what is pleasing to God. This is what the apostle John meant when he said: "But as many as received him, to them gave he power to become the sons of God, even to them that believe on his name" (John 1:12).

And this is what I had to do to find the peace and the joy and the freedom that I desired. Many times I had wanted to do the right thing, and many times I had even tried to do the right thing. Sometimes it even seemed to work—until I found myself doing the very thing I had said I wouldn't do and, conversely, not doing the things I had said I would do. This life of bondage continued until the day came when I went beyond desiring and working hard and decided to allow the Lord to will and to do in me His good pleasure. Then and only then did I discover what Jesus meant when He said, "If the Son therefore shall make you free, ye shall be free indeed" (John 8:36).

We don't really understand the power we have in the right use of choice. I certainly didn't. When I first chose to surrender my life to the Lord, there were wrong things, which I loved, in my life. All kinds of doubts and fears were going through my mind at the time. But I wanted real peace. I wanted real joy, real strength, real hope. I was tired of the transitory peace and momentary joy this world offers.

I came to realize that what this world calls strength is nothing but weakness, and the hope that worldly strength offers is as empty as the politician's promise to make this world a better place in which to live. I longed for the "abundant life" that Jesus said He came to give (John 10:10). This longing of my soul drove me to make the choice to surrender my life to the Lord in spite of my doubts and fears. In my desperation, I cried out in these words: "Lord, I want You to take control of my life, and do it now because I don't know if I can ever mean it this much again. You know I have wrong things in my life.

Things I can't even pray about right now because I'm afraid to give them up. But I'm not going to worry about those things because I believe You'll get me to the place where I'll want to give them up. So I'm asking You to take me and make me what I should be . . . and do it now!"

When I got up from that prayer, I believed that Jesus had heard and answered, so I acted on that belief. I threw away my cigarettes, my marijuana, and my heroin. And I haven't touched them since. I haven't even had a desire for them.

I agree with the statement I quoted earlier, which says that through the right exercise of the will an entire change can be made in the life. And it will work for you. By yielding your will to Christ, you ally yourself with the power that is above all principalities and powers.

The same thing happened with my drinking problem when I stopped making excuses for it and began to place my power of choice on the Lord's side. Since then I've learned that I should never make excuses for my sins, because that is giving Satan my will and makes victory impossible.

First Corinthians 10:13 says: "There hath no temptation taken you but such as is common to man: but God is faithful, who will not suffer you to be tempted above that ye are able; but will with the temptation also make a way of escape, that ye may be able to bear it."

When we choose to believe that promise, despite how we may feel at the time, and ask the Lord for strength to accomplish it, we'll find that He will provide the "way of escape" and keep us from falling. But if we choose to give in to doubt and begin to make excuses, we will surely fall.

"Satan is jubilant when he hears the professed followers of Christ making excuses for their deformity of character. It is these excuses that lead to sin. There is no excuse for sinning" *(The Desire of Ages,* p. 311).

But there's still one more element to understand about the cross experience. *When* should we lift it? If you don't take the next step and get this understanding, you'll find yourself right back at square one.

I thought I had it made as long as I used my power of choice in the *right way.* Little did I know that the *right time* was just as important. I didn't realize this until I found myself getting tired of the job of trying to make sure that each time temptation arose I would surrender my choice to Jesus' control. Do you realize how many times during the course of a day you're tempted to do wrong—especially when you have as many bad habits as I had?

I was doing pretty well at first, but slowly I slipped right back into working hard to do right. God pointed me to this statement: "All true obedience comes from the heart. It was heart work with Christ. And if we consent, He will so identify Himself with our thoughts and aims, so blend our hearts and minds into conformity to His will, that when obeying Him we shall be but carrying out our own impulses. The will, refined and sanctified, will find its highest delight in doing His service. When we know God as it is our privilege to know Him, our life will be a life of continual obedience. Through an appreciation of the character of Christ, through communion with God, sin will become hateful to us" *(ibid.,* p. 668).

What I was experiencing was not impulsive, and it was beginning to be not so continual. As I began to pray about how to have this kind of walk, God directed me to the sanctuary tapes I referred to earlier, and they gave me a deeper understanding of Hebrews 4:16: "Let us therefore come boldly unto the throne of grace, that we may obtain mercy, and find grace to help in time of need."

Most of us understand this passage to mean we're to come to the throne *at the time of need.* But this is *not* what the text says. It says to come to the throne to "obtain mercy," and *then* we'll find the grace to help in the time of need. If we wait until the time of need to come to the throne, it will be too late. No wonder I was using so much effort to give my will to Jesus! I was fighting the *right* battle at the *wrong* time. If we wait until the moment of temptation to give our choice to Jesus, that means He didn't have our choice before the temptation came. It's like trying to change drivers while the car is going 120 miles an hour. It's very difficult, if not impossible. But if you start out with the right driver, the problem is solved.

Hebrews 4:15 lets us know that Jesus understands our feelings of weakness because He too was tempted "in all points" just like we are, *but* He did not sin—ever. In other words, He always gave His will to the Father. What was His secret? Mark 1:35 gives us our first clue: "And in the morning, rising up a great while before day, he went out, and departed into a solitary place, and there prayed."

Jesus did not wait until He was in need to pray. He went to the throne "in the morning, rising a great while before day," and as a result, He had grace to help Him "in time of need." Here was the secret to resisting temptation when it came upon Him, no matter how strongly or how suddenly it came. He didn't have to struggle with giving His will to the Father at the time of temptation. It was as natural for Him to do this as it is for the sunflower to turn toward the life-giving rays of the sun. He did not have to work hard to think of a text of Scripture to quote in order to rebuke Satan. It came to Him naturally at the time He needed it and on a continual basis. Obedience for Him was internal, not external. It came from the heart, and so it will be with us when we learn to take up our cross not only as He did but also when He did.

Before we get too carried away with how easy it was for Jesus, we need to look at Hebrews 5:7, 8, which says: "Who in the days of his flesh, when he had offered up prayers and supplications with strong crying and tears unto him that was able to save him from death, and was heard in that he feared; though he were a Son, yet learned he obedience by the things which he suffered."

Jesus can truly understand our struggles because He had to struggle also. But His struggle was not at the time of temptation. It was early in the morning before daybreak and sometimes all night. It says that He did this because "he feared."

What did Jesus have to fear? Wasn't He divine? Yes, but He chose to empty Himself of His divinity and become one of us (Phil. 2:5-10). He had to learn obedience through suffering just like we do, because He came in the "likeness of sinful flesh" (Rom. 8:3).

Therefore, He feared to trust the weakness of His flesh because He knew He would fall. So every morning, a great while before the time of need, He would agonize in prayer with "strong crying and tears unto him that was able to save him from death," not the death of the cross, but the death of sin. And He was heard.

This was Jesus' secret, and when we begin to fight the right battle of surrendering the will at the right time—early in the morning—we too will find the grace to help us in our time of need and be saved from the death of sin.

Here is the only way we'll ever experience impulsive and continual obedience. Sin will then become hateful to us, and our testimony will be: "I delight to do thy will, O my God: yea, thy law is within my heart" (Ps. 40:8).

We now need to look at the process involved in surrender.

Discussion Questions

1. What must we understand before we can truly surrender? (p. 61)
2. What is the "true force of the will"? (p. 61)
3. What does it mean to give Jesus your will? (pp. 61, 62)
4. Why must we give the will to Jesus? (p. 64)
5. What happens when we make excuses for our sins? Why? (p. 64)
6. Does it make any difference when I give my will to the Lord? Why? (pp. 65-67)
7. Did Jesus have to struggle with giving His will to the Father at the time of temptation? Why? (p. 67)

Chapter Five

The Process of Surrender

For the final chapter it might be appropriate to bring together all the points we've learned about surrender and see how they can be applied in our daily living. But first we need to summarize the five major tenets presented in this book.

1. **What**—The daily lift represents daily surrendering the control of every area of our lives to Jesus.

2. **Why**—Everything we do, even our righteous deeds, is self-centered and therefore sinful.

3. **Where the problem lies**—Whenever we are struggling with our daily lift, it is because we are choosing to believe one or more of Satan's three major lies. This makes us afraid to surrender control of our lives to Jesus.

4. **How**—The way to surrender is on every issue to put the will on the side of the Lord. This is accomplished by *choosing* to believe God's Word and *allowing* Jesus to work in us to will and to do His will.

5. **When**—The right time to make that choice is *before* the time of need. We must go to the throne of grace early in the morning in order to have the grace to help us in the time of need.

Now we can look at how to apply these five tenets.

Tenets 5 and 2

As stated earlier, too many Christians are trying to

fight the right battle at the wrong time. As a result, many of us find ourselves doing the very thing we said we would not do and not doing the things we said we would do. *If we are to be successful in surrendering, we must do it at the right time.*

We have already discovered that Jesus got up a "great while before day" and went to a quiet place to pray (Mark 1:35). But it's also important to know how to get up. Isaiah 50:4, 5 gives us that information: "The Lord God hath given me the tongue of the learned, that I should know how to speak a word in season to him that is weary: *he wakeneth morning by morning,* he wakeneth mine ear to hear as the learned. The Lord God hath opened mine ear, and I was not rebellious, neither turned away back."

Christians see in this text a prophecy of Jesus' experience. He depended on the Father to awaken Him daily to give Him wisdom as well as strength for that day. This is to be our experience also. He was our example in all things. If we'd begin allowing the Lord to awaken us every morning, we'd find the solution to the problem of not having enough time for a meaningful devotional life. When I say that we need to allow the Lord to wake us up, I'm not talking about giving us the gift of life. Instead, I'm talking about Him acting as our alarm clock. This is why the text said: "He wakeneth morning by morning, he wakeneth mine ear to hear as the learned. The Lord God hath opened mine ear, and I was not rebellious, neither turned away back."

"Everyone needs to have a personal experience in obtaining a knowledge of the will of God. We must individually hear Him speaking to the heart. When every other voice is hushed, and in quietness we wait before Him, the silence of the soul makes more distinct the voice of God" *(The Desire of Ages,* p. 363).

The Lord wants to wake us up to speak to us, and if we don't rebel by turning over and going back to sleep, He'll speak to us personally, giving us the wisdom and strength we need for that day. This is what Jesus was talking about when He said: "But seek ye first the kingdom of God, and his righteousness; and all these things shall be added unto you. Take therefore no thought for the morrow: for the morrow shall take thought for the things of itself. Sufficient unto the day is the evil thereof" (Matt. 6:33, 34).

The first thing that should be on our minds in the morning is seeking God in order to receive strength and wisdom for that day. Too often we wake up with the combined worries of yesterday's, today's, and tomorrow's problems on our minds, and the first thing we seek is how to solve them. If only we'd learn to do as Jesus did, we'd find that as we seek *first* the kingdom of God in order to receive power to do His righteous will all our worries will be taken care of.

When we allow Him to awaken us each morning, He'll give us the wisdom we need for that day's challenges and the strength necessary to meet those challenges. That which we cannot do will not worry us, because we have received assurance that day from the Lord that He is working all things together for our good. This is how we can have the perfect peace that Isaiah 26:3 says comes as a result of keeping our minds "stayed" on the Lord—because we seek first the kingdom of God to do His will.

Therefore, I suggest that whatever you use to awaken you in the morning continue to use it, but tonight before going to bed ask the Lord to awaken you with Him on your mind. Do this for at least a week. I guarantee you that if not on the first night, at least before the week is out, God will have awakened you before your usual time—with Him on your mind. The problem won't be with God's awakening you. The problem will usually be with your response to God's wake-up call.

You'll find that God will give you plenty of time to bring your burdens to Him. This means that He'll wake you up earlier than most of you would normally choose to be awakened (both literally and figuratively). He'll respect your power of choice, of course. You can choose to give your will to Him by making a decision to get up, or you can choose to rebel by deciding it's too early (excuse)—you need just a few more winks.

Here is where number 2 comes in. When the Lord wakes you up and you feel like going back to sleep, remember that you are a hopeless slave to sin and that if you don't get up and receive God's wisdom and power, you'll be misused and abused by Satan because of your weakness.

That's what I do, and when I tell myself this truth, it sets me free to use the power of choice in the right way. I've been allowing the Lord to awaken me for more than five years now, and I always have time for the Lord and everything else I must do that day.

Tenet 4

Now that we have applied tenets 5 and 2, we're ready to start giving our will to the Lord. This brings us to the *how-to* of surrendering. Contrary to what many of us believe, we cannot give the Lord control over our lives in a general way. We cannot just get down on our knees and say "Lord, take control of my life" and then rush out the door. If this were all that was necessary, then Jesus need not have spent hours, sometimes the entire night, in prayer with "strong crying and tears." But He did this because He knew that if He failed to give God the Father control in each and every area of His life, Satan would gain the victory over Him. This is what He feared. So He would spend hours at the throne of grace, receiving mercy, so that He would find "grace to help in time of need."

That's why Jesus could say: "I can of mine own self do nothing: as I hear, I judge: and my judgment is just; because I seek not mine own will, but the will of the Father which hath sent me" (John 5:30).

Jesus took everything concerning His life to the Father in prayer and surrendered His will to the Father's on every issue. And so He could say that everything He did was done by the power and authority of His Father.

"As one with us, a sharer in our needs and weaknesses, He was wholly dependent upon God, and in the secret place of prayer He sought divine strength, that He might go forth braced for duty and trial. In a world of sin Jesus endured struggles and torture of soul. In communion with God He could unburden the sorrows that were crushing Him. Here He found comfort and joy. . . .

"As a man He supplicated the throne of God till His humanity was charged with a heavenly current that should connect humanity with divinity. . . . His experience is to be ours" *(The Desire of Ages*, p. 363). I agree with the author that Jesus' experience is to be ours. When we begin to pray like Jesus, we'll begin to live like Him.

I used to wonder how Jesus could spend so much time in prayer. I wondered what He found to talk about that would take hours. I'd try to do it, and after about 15 minutes I'd run out of things to say. The exception to this was when I was heavy with a burden, then I could last about 30 minutes, most of which was vain repetition. It wasn't until I encountered the sanctuary model for prayer that I understood how to really pray as Jesus did.

I won't go into detail about what I mean by the sanctuary model for prayer, but I'll share what I feel will be helpful.

When God gave the Israelites the instructions to build

Him a sanctuary, He said: "And let them make me a sanctuary; that I may dwell among them. According to all that I shew thee, after the pattern of the tabernacle, and the pattern of all the instruments thereof, even so shall ye make it" (Ex. 25:8, 9).

This sanctuary that God showed to Moses was a "pattern," or copy, of *the* tabernacle. The book of Hebrews tells us what tabernacle the Old Testament sanctuary was a copy of: "Now of the things which we have spoken this is the sum: We have such an high priest, who is set on the right hand of the throne of the Majesty in the heavens; a minister of the sanctuary, and of the true tabernacle, which the Lord pitched, and not man" (Heb. 8:1, 2).

The Old Testament sanctuary and the services that were given with it were a copy of the "true tabernacle" that is in heaven. In the services of the earthly sanctuary, God portrayed the complete plan of salvation. Everything we need to know for our salvation is taught in the services of the Old Testament sanctuary, including how to pray. (I go into detail in a seminar that I give on this topic.) But this isn't just any prayer. This prayer will bring you into God's very throne room, where you can actually feel His presence and experience His power charging your feeble humanity with His divinity. This is the kind of praying Jesus did.

I had a good prayer life before I learned the sanctuary model of prayer. (By the way, the sanctuary model of prayer follows the same outline as the Lord's Prayer.) But when I began to follow the steps in the sanctuary model, my walk with the Lord became much more intimate. My life became much more victorious. I entered into another level of spirituality. The spiritual level I had been on was fairly good when measured by human standards. This fact made me skeptical about accepting the possibility that there was a better way to pray than I was already practicing. But I'm glad to say that my sincere desire to become more like Jesus overruled my spiritual pride. Once I tried it, I knew that the sanctuary model of prayer was of the Lord.

Let me share with you the basic outline I follow in giving the Lord total control of every area of my life.

No matter how bad I may feel when I start or how much I may want to talk about a pressing need or problem, I choose to praise the Lord first. I do this because it takes my mind off myself and focuses it on the Lord. As my mind begins to think on God's goodness and His past blessings, a peace begins to come over me, which is what Isaiah 26:3 says will happen. This is why the Israelites were told to enter the courts of the sanctuary in this manner. "Enter into his gates with thanksgiving, and into his courts with praise" (Ps. 100:4).

In order to make this praise genuine, because there are times when I don't feel like praising Him first, I claim the promise in Isaiah 61:3, which says that the Lord will give us the "garment of praise for the spirit of heaviness." In doing this, I'm choosing to allow Jesus to work in me both to will and to do of His good pleasure in spite of the way I feel at the time. The Holy Spirit takes the Word of God and writes it on my heart. Jesus said: "It is the spirit that quickeneth; the flesh profiteth nothing: the words that I speak unto you, they are spirit, and they are life" (John 6:63). The Word then becomes alive in me as Jesus works in me both to will and to do His good pleasure.

Notice what Ellen White says concerning this text of Scripture. "In every command and in every promise of the Word of God is the power, the very life of God, by which the command may be fulfilled and the promise realized. He who by faith receives the word is receiving the very life and character of God" *(Christ's Object Lessons,* p. 38).

Because the power of God is in His Word, I claim one

of His promises or commands at every step in the process and give Him my consent to make it part of me. Then I can truly say that I can do all things through Christ who strengthens me (Phil. 4:13).

The sanctuary model lets me know that after praise comes confession of all my sins so that I might receive forgiveness and cleansing. This is represented by the altar of burnt sacrifice. During the time of Moses the Israelite priest daily offered an innocent lamb whole on the altar as a sacrifice for sin. This represented Israel giving all its sins to Jesus, the Lamb of God. So the altar of burnt offerings represents surrender to Jesus, because sin is a choice not to surrender to the Lord's authority.

To give Jesus our sins is the same as giving Him our choice to surrender to His authority in that area of our lives. As the sacrifice of Moses' time was offered up whole, so too must our surrender be whole and complete. We must lay our all on the altar of sacrifice so that the Lord's authority may rule in every area of our lives.

To accomplish this, I start with the prayer of Psalm 139:23, 24, which says: "Search me, O God, and know my heart: try me, and know my thoughts: and see if there be any wicked way in me, and lead me in the way everlasting."

After repeating the prayer of Psalm 139:23, 24, I reflect on the past 24 hours of my life. This allows the Lord to reveal "any wicked way in me." During this time God shows me more than just my sinful acts; He shows me the sinful thoughts and also the motives that generated the sinful acts.

Although I focus on the past 24 hours of my life, I leave myself open to whatever God's Spirit wants to reveal, because this is the time God deals with the root causes of my sins. At times He has shown me things concerning my early childhood—things that shed light on why I feel the way I feel and do the things I do. These revelations have proven to be necessary for me to repent effectively and gain the victory over particular sins.

For example, I was struggling with overcoming a problem in the area of sexual lust. No matter how much I prayed, I just could not seem to get the victory over this particular problem. I was constantly cherishing thoughts of sexual lust. Although I had not actually committed the act of adultery, I was constantly struggling with it and had come very close to committing it on several occasions. I thought about what Jesus said: "Ye have heard that it was said by them of old time, Thou shalt not commit adultery: but I say unto you, That whosoever looketh on a woman to lust after her hath committed adultery with her already in his heart" (Matt. 5:27, 28). I realized that if I did not allow the Lord to deal with the lust in my heart, it would eventually reveal itself in the act of adultery.

In order to get to the root cause of my problem, the Lord took me back to the time in my life when I had begun to formulate wrong ideas concerning sexuality. In my morning "sessions" with the Lord (I call them sessions because at these times He is my psychiatrist), He showed me how different events at key points in my life had shaped my ideas on how to use my sexuality. Over a period of time, He showed me that my problem with sexual lust was not my desire for sex, but rather it was motivated by my desire to feel powerful and in control.

This revelation let me know that my sin was not in the area of "the lust of the flesh" but in the area of "the pride of life." (First John 2:16 says that the three categories of sin are the lust of the flesh, the lust of the eyes, and the pride of life.) I then began to focus on my ego needs rather than on my sexual needs. I asked the Lord to take away my sinful concept of power and control and give me the right concept so that He could satisfy these needs in a way that was pleasing in His sight.

Since that time, I no longer struggle with not committing adultery because I no longer cherish lustful thoughts. This does not mean that thoughts of sexual lust no longer come into my mind, because they do, but I immediately give those thoughts to the Lord. I do this by asking the Lord to take the thought away, and it goes away immediately. This happens because the Lord has removed the root cause of the problem. Lest anyone get the idea this happened overnight, I must point out that even though victory is now immediate, the removal of the root problem occurred over a period of time.

Though the Lord sometimes finds it necessary to take me back to earlier periods in my life, more often than not He just deals with the past 24 hours. To make sure I allow the Lord to search every area of my life, I follow an outline that I'll share with you along with a brief explanation of what I focus on at each step as I claim texts of Scripture.

Will—After pausing to allow the Lord to show me whether or not I've been rebellious in this area during the past 24 hours, I claim Philippians 2:13: "For it is God which worketh in you both to will and to do of his good pleasure."

Mind—Here I deal with my thoughts. The main text of Scripture I claim is "Casting down imaginations, and every high thing that exalteth itself against the knowledge of God, and bringing into captivity every thought to the obedience of Christ" (2 Cor. 10:5).

Body—At this point, I focus on my appetites and my passions. For my appetite (eating), I claim: "Whether therefore ye eat, or drink, or whatsoever ye do, do all to the glory of God" (1 Cor. 10:31).

For my passions, I claim Galatians 5:22, 23: "But the fruit of the Spirit is love, joy, peace, longsuffering, gentleness, goodness, faith, meekness, temperance: against such there is no law."

Time—My focus here is how I've used my time and whether or not I've sought and followed God's plans for my life or my own. The scripture I claim is: "See then that ye walk circumspectly, not as fools, but as wise, redeeming the time, because the days are evil. Wherefore be ye not unwise, but understanding what the will of the Lord is" (Eph. 5:15-17).

Money—Here I deal with my finances. I go over my financial decisions past, present, and future to make sure that God was—and is—leading in them. My favorite text here is Matthew 6:31, 33, in which Jesus said: "Therefore take no thought, saying, What shall we eat? or, What shall we drink? or, Wherewithal shall we be clothed?" "But seek ye first the kingdom of God, and his righteousness; and all these things shall be added unto you."

Summary—At this point I ask God to make me a faithful steward in every area of my life. I then claim: "Moreover it is required in stewards, that a man be found faithful" (1 Cor. 4:2).

That's the outline I follow. As the Lord reveals "the wicked way in me," I repent and ask for forgiveness and cleansing.

After repentance I talk to the Lord about my needs and concerns in specific areas of my life. I tell Him just how I feel. I don't try to hide anything from Him because He knows it already. "Well," you might ask, "why tell Him then?" I tell Him, not because I want to inform Him, but because I want to lay all my burdens on Him. Instead of laying my burdens on another person who is already struggling with his or her own problems and can only sympathize with me, I take them to Jesus. He not only sympathizes with me, but also He gives me the strength and the wisdom to do what I need to do. Even more important, He gives me the patience I need to wait for Him to do what only He can do. "He giveth power to the faint; and to them that have no might he increaseth strength. Even the youths shall faint and be weary, and the young men shall utterly fall: but they that wait upon the Lord shall renew their strength; they shall mount up with wings as eagles; they shall run, and not be weary; and they shall walk, and not faint" (Isa. 40:29-31).

The Hebrew word that is interpreted "wait" connotes the idea of waiting in anticipation or waiting with hope for something to happen. So when I "wait upon" the Lord, I anticipate His forthcoming blessing. I will receive joy that will cause me to mount up with eagle's wings, strength that will enable me not to become weary of running this race, and hope that will help me not to faint as I walk in the footsteps of Jesus. This is why I take everything to the Lord in my prayer. It is my way of giving my problems and perplexities to Him—how I surrender all.

I search, repent, and surrender at each step in the outline. It's important to deal with each area. If we neglect any of them, that particular area of our lives is not surrendered to His control and thus becomes sinful no matter how many good things we may do. Satan can have a field day with this unsurrendered area because as human beings we are powerless when it comes to resisting him. By failing to surrender even one area of our lives, Satan can gain control. It thus becomes clear why it is that one sin can cause us to be lost.

Let's examine more closely why it isn't possible to have true victory in our lives until and unless we surrender every area of our lives to God.

Appetite is an area I cover while dealing with surrendering my body to the Lord's control. Happy Christians think they can eat and drink whatever, whenever, however, and wherever they want. The scripture they love is: "For every creature of God is good, and nothing to be refused, if it be received with thanksgiving" (1 Tim. 4:4).

At the other extreme are the Martyrs who pride themselves on how they deny self of the things that they love in order to be the holy vessel the Lord requires them to be. One of their favorite texts is: "If any man defile the temple of God, him shall God destroy; for the temple of God is holy, which temple ye are" (1 Cor. 3:17).

Sandwiched between these two extremes are the rational Happy Martyrs, who do not agree with the concept that one can eat anything one wishes. They realize that the Bible says that certain things defile the body and that 1 Timothy 4:5 says food is sanctified not only by prayer but also by the Word. Therefore, they won't eat anything the Word clearly condemns as unclean or drink anything it says they shouldn't. This is the Martyr part. But the Happy part says that other than that, they can eat and drink whatever, whenever, however, and wherever they want. They admit that this isn't the healthiest way to live (Martyr part), but they don't feel that God cares about that too much as long as they are sincere (Happy part).

None of these views will ever lead such people to live as admonished in 1 Corinthians 10:31: "Whether therefore ye eat, or drink, or whatsoever ye do, do all to the glory of God." In order to have this kind of experience, one must be fully surrendered to the Lord's control in this area. Such isn't the case for any of these types of Christians. The Martyrs are too busy glorying in the fact that they are denying themselves. The Happy Christians are too busy glorying in their freedom to eat and drink as they please. The Happy Martyrs are too busy glorying in their rationale that keeps them from going to either extreme. But none of them is seeking to glorify God in whatever they eat or drink or do.

Galatians 5:24, 25 tells us that we must "crucify" our passions and lust in order to "walk in the Spirit." When we do this, we'll find ourselves not wanting to eat anything that will not be good or is unhealthy for us, even though we are free to do so. This will happen because we won't want to do anything in our bodies that will not glorify God.

Yet we won't have to deny ourselves of things we love, because *we will walk as the Spirit leads us, allowing the Lord to first work in us to will before we do.* As we "walk in the Spirit" our testimony will be: "I delight to do thy will, O my God: yea, thy law is within my heart" (Ps. 40:8).

I know that some may be afraid that following this outline for surrender will make the prayer life a routine. But it will be no more routine than meeting your daily needs. The purpose behind using an outline is that it affords you an organized way to surrender every area of your life to the Lord on a daily basis.

Because each day is different, so too what you and the Lord talk about in these areas will differ. You'll go through some areas quickly one day, but linger on them the next because of the need. But I caution you: Don't make going through this outline a work and become a slave to it. It's only a tool to enhance your fellowship with the Lord. If it doesn't enable you to do that, it's no good, no matter how good it is!

Tenet 3

Suppose you come to an area in this outline that you find hard to surrender to the Lord. Again, I will use the area of appetite because it's the strongest passion we have, making it the hardest area for many of us to surrender. I know it was hard for me at first, because I was still believing Satan's lie instead of believing the Word of the Lord.

It wasn't long after my initial conversion that the Lord brought to my attention the importance my eating and drinking habits played in my Christian growth. While studying the Bible, I came across 1 Corinthians 6:19, 20: "What? know ye not that your body is the temple of the Holy Ghost which is in you, which ye have of God, and ye are not your own? For ye are bought with a price: therefore glorify God in your body, and in your spirit, which are God's."

God was speaking directly to me. The Holy Spirit opened my eyes to the truth that my body isn't mine. It, as well as my spirit, was bought with a high price. Jesus gave up everything He had in glory and came down here to die a cruel and shameful death on the cross in order to redeem both my body and spirit. In light of this, my body belongs to Him, and He expects me to glorify Him with it.

As I read 1 Corinthians 10:31 I realized that this meant more than sexual purity. It also included whatever I ate or drank. After this revelation, I began to read *The Ministry of Healing* and *Counsels on Diet and Foods,* by Ellen G. White. I also began to read as many of the health magazines and articles as I could possibly lay my hands on. The more I read, the more I realized how much my eating and drinking habits do affect my spiritual life.

I was on fire for the Lord, so I tried to put into practice all that I was learning. But I was trying to accomplish all this in the strength of my own sinful flesh, because I hadn't yet learned how to daily surrender this area of my life to the Lord's control. Needless to say, I went through a lot of changes until the Lord delivered me by giving me a better understanding of righteousness by faith. (I say "better" because I had yet to come to a full understanding of it.)

As my understanding grew, I began to depend on Jesus more, and consequently I made tremendous strides. However, after a while my ability to continue this growth became stagnant because I limited the Lord when it came to certain things. I justified my lack of faith by saying things such as "I'm not ready for that yet" or "It's not time to give up that yet" or "There are other things more important to deal with than that" or "I'm doing better than so and so." And so it went until the Lord brought me to the sanctuary model of prayer.

As I began to deal specifically with each area of my life and allowed the Lord to take control, He began to reveal truth to me on a much deeper level. I began to see the hidden thoughts and intents of my deceitful heart. I began to see the lies that had bound me with fear, and as I turned from them and chose to allow Jesus to empower me, I was set free.

Let me illustrate how this happens by sharing another personal experience. One day after having my prayer session with the Lord, I went into the kitchen to prepare my breakfast. At this time I was eating only two meals a day. I didn't drink anything with my meals, and I didn't eat anything between my meals. I had been a vegetarian for about 15 years. I exercised almost daily. In short, I could have felt pretty satisfied with where I was in that area of my life, and to a certain degree, I did.

But as I began to get my breakfast together, the Lord spoke to me about my use—or should I say misuse?—of sugar. (Notice that this revelation came to me after my session with the Lord. It occurred at that particular time because once you've surrendered a particular area to the Lord, you're open to His impressions concerning that area of your life all during that day.)

The Lord showed me that my use of sugar (especially in the area of sweets) was hindering the growth He wanted to accomplish in me. As He did, I began to think about what I would have to give up, and how much I loved some of those things, and how miserable my life would be without them. I thought about how restrictive my diet would be if I did what I was impressed to do, and how people would see me as some kind of strange fanatic.

All this caused me to become fearful and back away from what the Lord was leading me to do. I told the Lord that I didn't think I was ready to give Him total control of my diet yet, but then I asked Him to please be patient with me and not give up on me. (Of course, the Lord wasn't about to give up on me. He never gives up on us; rather, we give up on Him.) But though He didn't give up on me, what He did was to allow me to see the result of drawing back from following Him all the way.

When I began to eat my dessert that Sabbath, I went out of control. The Sabbath meal at our house is usually special. My wife really knows how to put it together in the kitchen, especially when it comes to desserts. Despite that, I had been able to limit myself to one or, at the most, two pieces (of course, I mean good-sized pieces) of 7-Up cake (one of my favorites). But on this particular Sabbath I was totally out of control.

I'm not going to satisfy your curiosity by telling you how much I ate, but I'll tell you this much. After the orgy was over, I sat there like a stuffed pig, thoroughly disgusted with myself. At that time the Lord and I had a little talk as He impressed my mind with this question: "Greg, are you satisfied with yourself?"

I said, "No, Lord."

He then asked, "Are you ready to trust Me now?"

And I said, "Yes, Lord!"

At that time I made a choice to surrender to His control and do as He had impressed me. Since that day I have not had any desire to eat desserts made with sugar. This is not to say that eating sugar is a sin. I am only sharing how the Lord dealt with me in that area. Of course, I must make the decision to surrender my appetite to the Lord on a daily basis in order to continue to walk in this victory. I've done this faithfully, because I've come to firmly believe in tenet 2. I know that on my own I'm a slave to my appetite. My only hope of freedom is in taking up my cross daily and following Jesus.

Do you see how my fears had limited me from experiencing the power of the Lord in that area of my life and how He led me to the truth about those fears?

I had chosen to believe Satan's lies. I believed that if I surrendered to the Lord's will concerning the use of sugar, I'd not be happy and would lose control over that area of my life. I also felt I'd be limiting my freedom to be the kind of person I wanted to be.

But the Lord showed me, in the way best suited for my personality, that there was only one way I was going to be truly happy with myself while still being in control of my life and being free to become the kind of person I truly wanted to be. That way was to let Him have full control of my appetite. Then He could work in me to will and do His good pleasure.

Since I surrendered—and continue to surrender—I'm truly happy. I've never had so much control over my appetite in all my life. I'm no longer a slave to sweets. God has restored my dominion. I can now say no to sweets and have no regrets. But more important than all these things is that it has enhanced my spiritual life. My walk with the Lord is much closer now because my mind is clearer.

The Lord meant it when He said: "If the Son therefore shall make you free, ye shall be free indeed" (John 8:36).

"How willing is Christ to take possession of the soul temple if we will let Him! . . . Then why does He not enter? It is because the love of sin has closed the door of the heart. As soon as we consent to give sin up, to acknowledge our guilt, the barrier is removed between the soul and the Saviour" (Ellen G. White, *Selected Messages,* book 1, p. 325).

If you've been struggling with your daily lift in the

area of diet or in any other area, don't be afraid to trust Him. Make a choice right now to give Him control of whatever it is, be it your money, time, will, thoughts, or passions. Only then will you begin to experience what the Lord has promised: "Delight thyself also in the Lord; and he shall give thee the desires of thine heart" (Ps. 37:4).

Tenet 1

In 2 Timothy 1:12 the apostle Paul professes his confidence in the Lord's ability to keep him: "For I know whom I have believed, and am persuaded that he is able to keep that which I have committed unto him against that day."

Each of us must have this same complete confidence. Don't allow anything to take it away. For it's our confidence in the Lord's ability to keep that which we have committed to Him that gives us continual victory. "For whatsoever is born of God overcometh the world: and this is the victory that overcometh the world, even our faith" (1 John 5:4).

"It is not our efforts that bring victory, it is seeing God behind the promise, and believing and trusting Him. Grasp by faith the hand of infinite power. The Lord is faithful who has promised" (Ellen G. White, in *Review and Herald,* Dec. 29, 1910).

As we go about our day, trusting in the Lord's ability to keep us, we'll find He is able to do just that. Temptations that once caused us to stumble will be overcome with ease because God will be working in us through the indwelling of the Spirit. When we need to pray, the Holy Spirit will put a prayer on our lips. Anything we need to live victoriously will be given at the precise time we need it because we have already been to the throne of grace and received mercy. This is what it means to "walk in the Spirit." "This I say then, Walk in the Spirit, and ye shall not fulfil the lust of the flesh" (Gal. 5:16).

In other words, when we're fully under the Holy Spirit's control, we'll have no desire to sin, because this is contrary to the Spirit. Our obedience will be impulsive and continual, as was stated in an earlier quotation. "And ye know that he was manifested to take away our sins; and in him is no sin. Whosoever abideth in him sinneth not: whosoever sinneth hath not seen him, neither known him" (1 John 3:5, 6).

Jesus didn't sin, and when we've been crucified with Christ, He is able to keep us from sinning. "Do not settle down in Satan's easy chair, and say that there is no use, you cannot cease to sin, that there is no power in you to overcome. There is no power in you apart from Christ, but it is your privilege to have Christ abiding in your heart by faith, and He can overcome sin in you, when you cooperate with His efforts" (Ellen G. White, *Our High Calling*, p. 76).

Having said all this, one might think I'm saying that to follow my surrender prayer outline will result in one's becoming sinlessly perfect. Am I advocating holy flesh? If not, is it possible for one to be fully surrendered to God's authority and still be a sinner? If so, how can this be?

First, let me be clear on this one point. There is no such thing as holy flesh. The Scriptures tell us that the flesh is weak. Jesus said: "Watch and pray, that ye enter not into temptation: the spirit indeed is willing, but the flesh is weak" (Matt. 26:41). And in John 6:63 Jesus tells us that "the flesh profiteth nothing."

Paul put it this way: "For I know that in me (that is, in my flesh,) dwelleth no good thing: for to will is present with me; but how to perform that which is good I find not. . . . But I see another law in my members, warring against the law of my mind, and bringing me into captivity to the law of sin which is in my members. O wretched man that I am! who shall deliver me from the body of this death?" (Rom. 7:18-24).

In Romans 12 Paul says: "I beseech you therefore, brethren, by the mercies of God, that ye present your bodies a living sacrifice, holy, acceptable unto God, which is your reasonable service" (verse 1).

How are we to do this? He goes on to say: "And be not conformed to this world: but be ye transformed by the renewing of your mind, that ye may prove what is that good, and acceptable, and perfect, will of God" (verse 2).

We are urged to renew our minds, but we aren't given any instructions on how to make flesh holy. Therefore according to the Scriptures, there can be no holy flesh. There is no such thing as holy flesh.

Now let's address the questions Is it possible for one to be fully surrendered to the authority of God over his or her life and still be a sinner? If so, how can this be?

Let's look at 1 John 3:6 again. Only this time we need to focus on the second half of the verse: "Whosoever sinneth hath not seen him, neither known him."

What does it mean when it says if you sin you have not seen Him, neither known Him? Did not Peter see Jesus? Yet he sinned, and so have all of the Lord's followers before and since—even the most faithful ones, such as Abraham, Jacob, Moses, and Paul. So it cannot be saying that if we sin, we haven't literally seen Jesus. Neither can it mean that if we sin, we aren't converted.

We can begin to solve this mystery by looking at Jesus' claim in John 14:6 that He is the truth. In John 8:32, He said: "Ye shall know the truth, and the truth will set you free," and then in verse 36 He said: "If the Son shall make you free." Jesus is the truth, and the truth is Jesus. When you don't know the truth, you don't know Jesus, and when you know Jesus, you know the truth. Therefore, when you sin, there's some truth you haven't yet seen.

This means that you don't know the power of Jesus in that area of your life because error and truth, sin and righteousness, Satan and Jesus, cannot occupy the same place at the same time.

There are two reasons for not knowing truth. One is that you've made a conscious choice not to know it. This is done by neglecting to learn the truths God has made available to you or by refusing to learn these truths. Notice what the Lord says will be the result of this choice: "My people are destroyed for lack of knowledge: because thou hast rejected knowledge, I will also reject thee" (Hosea 4:6).

The saying "What you don't know, won't hurt you" doesn't seem to hold water in light of this scripture. Not only can what you don't know hurt you, it can also cause you to be lost. When you reject the truth—either by neglect or refusal—you are rejecting Jesus, the Saviour. Thus, rejection is one way not to know truth.

But this way does not apply to those who are surrendering control of everything daily. To these, Jesus says: "And ye shall know the truth, and the truth shall make you free" (John 8:32).

This lack of knowledge doesn't come from an unwillingness to know the truth. Instead, it comes from a lack of opportunity to know it. The attitude of those who are surrendering daily isn't one of rebellion against the truth, but of sincere desire not only to know it but also to live it. Otherwise they would not be surrendering daily. To this kind of ignorance Acts 17:30 applies: "And the times of this ignorance God winked at; but now commandeth all men every where to repent."

There's no guilt with this kind of ignorance because the light of truth hasn't been known or seen. But those who are surrendering daily won't stay in ignorance of truth. They'll be led to more and more truth, because they are "walking in the Spirit." It is the Holy Spirit's job to guide them into "all truth" (John 16:13). And so they're given life more abundantly. The more truth they possess, the more they know of Jesus, who is life.

You can now see how it's possible to be surrendering fully every day and still sin. This doesn't occur because Jesus is unable to keep that which we have committed to Him, but because there are still some things in our lives that we haven't yet committed to Him because of ignorance.

When we first come to the Lord, we are full of sin (self). There are things in our lives that are hidden deep in the subconscious mind. We don't consciously know about these things, yet they strongly influence the way we act. Hebrews 12:15 calls these hidden sins the "root of bitterness" because they're the source of many other sins we commit.

Sometimes we come up against certain sins we just cannot seem to get the victory over. We pray about them, but our prayers seem to be of no avail. As a result, we doubt our sincerity. But the problem isn't one of sincerity, but of ignorance. A prime example of this ignorance is the problem I had with lustful thoughts. I didn't know the real causes of my sin. This is why we are told: "But grow in grace, and in the knowledge of our Lord and Saviour Jesus Christ" (2 Peter 3:18).

In John 16:12, 13, Jesus reveals how He will lead us in this growth in grace and knowledge: "I have yet many things to say unto you, but ye cannot bear them now. Howbeit when he, the Spirit of truth, is come, he will guide you into all truth."

Jesus did not reveal everything to His original disciples because they would not have been able to bear it all. They were not ready to hear all of it in their present state. So it is with us. If the Lord were to reveal all the truth about ourselves to us at one time, we wouldn't be able to stand it. So He tenderly guides us to more and more truth as we grow in His grace.

"But the path of the just is as a shining light, that shineth more and more unto the perfect day" (Prov. 4:18). As the Lord sheds more light, we begin to see those hidden sins, those "roots of bitterness," that have caused us to stumble time and time again. As we begin to see these sins, we have a choice to make. We either choose to reject the light by making excuses for these hidden sins, or we choose to surrender to the light by confessing those sins.

The choice to reject the light leads to condemnation (John 3:18, 19). The choice to surrender to the light leads to forgiveness and cleansing (1 John 1:6-10). As we continue to choose to surrender to the light as the Holy Spirit leads us, it will eventually bring us to experience what Paul talks about in Ephesians 4:13: "Till we all come in the unity of the faith, and of the knowledge of the Son of God, unto a perfect man, unto the measure of the stature of the fulness of Jesus Christ."

I believe that this is the finishing of the "mystery of God" that Revelation 10:7 says will take place just prior to the Lord's second coming. (See Revelation 11:15 for the timing of the seventh angel.)

"There are those who have known the pardoning love of Christ and who really desire to be children of God, yet they realize that their character is imperfect, their life faulty, and they are ready to doubt whether their hearts have been renewed by the Holy Spirit. To such I would say, Do not draw back in despair. We shall often have to bow down and weep at the feet of Jesus because of our shortcomings and mistakes, but we are not to be discouraged. Even if we are overcome by the enemy, we are not cast off, not forsaken and rejected of God. No; Christ is at the right hand of God, who also maketh intercession for us. . . . He desires to restore you to Himself, to see His own purity and holiness reflected in you. And if you will but yield yourself to Him, He that hath begun a good work in you will carry it forward to the day of Jesus Christ. . . .

"The closer you come to Jesus, the more faulty you will appear in your own eyes; for your vision will be clearer, and your imperfections will be seen in broad and distinct contrast to His perfect nature" (Ellen G. White, *Steps to Christ,* p. 64).

This is the result of daily surrender. So when you see sin in your life, don't get discouraged and lose your confidence in the Lord's ability to keep you. Remember tenet 1, and see it as a call to a deeper level of surrender. As you learn to do this, you'll advance from one level of perfection to the next. "First the blade, then the ear, after that the full corn in the ear" (Mark 4:28). When the harvest is fully ripe, the Lord will come to reap His harvest (Mark 4:29; Rev. 14:15).

This is biblical perfection, and it's the work of a lifetime, because as long as we are alive, it's our privilege to grow in the image of God.

"As through Jesus we enter into rest, heaven begins here. We respond to His invitation, Come, learn of Me, and in thus coming we begin the life eternal. Heaven is a ceaseless approaching to God through Christ. The longer we are in the heaven of bliss, the more and still more of glory will be opened to us; and the more we know of God, the more intense will be our happiness" *(The Desire of Ages,* p. 331).

Sin started in the heart of Lucifer because he desired to *be* God. This is impossible, for only God can be God. But as we take up our cross daily, it's our privilege to become more and more *like* God. This is really what we all long for, because this is the only thing that will truly satisfy the desires of our hearts. It's really what Lucifer wanted, but he chose to get it by exalting himself. He deceived Adam and Eve into believing that they had to get it this way too, and ever since that day humanity has been seeking to find peace and happiness by asserting and exalting self. Jesus came to show us that the right way is the way of the cross (Phil. 2:6-8), and we are admonished: "Let this mind be in you, which was also in Christ Jesus" (verse 5).

As we obey this admonition and take up our cross daily, we'll be able to say: "The Lord is my shepherd; I shall not want" (Ps. 23:1). And we'll know from our own experience that surrender is the only way to perfect peace and happiness.

Discussion Questions

1. What are the five major tenets discussed in this book? (p. 69)
2. What should be the first thing we do in the morning? (p. 70)
3. How can we solve the problem of not having enough quality time in the morning to spend with the Lord? How can Tenet 2 help us here? (pp. 71, 72)
4. Why is it important to start our prayers with praise? (p. 75)
5. Why is it important to claim a command or promise of the Bible in a specific manner? (pp. 75, 76)
6. Why is it important to deal with every area of your life in a specific manner? (p. 80)
7. What is the purpose of the outline? (p. 82)
8. What must we have in order to experience continual victory? (pp. 89, 90)
9. Do we have a desire to sin when we are fully under the control of the Holy Spirit? Why? (p. 90)
10. Is it possible to sin after you have surrendered all you know about yourself to the Lord's control? Why?

(pp. 91, 92)

11. What are the two reasons for not knowing the truth? (pp. 90-93)

12. Which one does God wink at? Why? (p. 90)

13. What makes it possible for God to show us more and more truth? Why? (pp. 91, 92)

14. To remain innocent, what must we do when God shows us our sins? (p. 93)

15. How is it possible to be perfect at every stage of growth in grace? (pp. 92, 93)

16. Why is sanctification the work of a lifetime? (p. 93)

17. What is the only way to perfect peace and happiness? (p. 93, 94)